# ROLLER COASTER ROMANCE

KATE MOSEMAN

Roller Coaster Romance
Copyright © 2019 by Kate Moseman

All rights reserved. No part of this book may be reproduced or used in any manner without written permission of the copyright owner except for the use of quotations in a book review.

This is a work of fiction. Names, characters, places, and incidents either are the product of the author's imagination or are used fictitiously. Any resemblance to actual persons, living or dead, events, or locales is entirely coincidental.

First Edition

Cover design by Rena Violet, coversbyviolet.com
Interior design by Stephanie Anderson, Alt 19 Publications

ISBN 978-0-9996594-8-9 (paperback)
ISBN 978-0-9996594-9-6 (ebook)

Fortunella Press

Subscribe to Kate Moseman's newsletter at

# *katemoseman.com*

for exclusive freebies,
and be the first to know about upcoming releases!

*For Ginger*

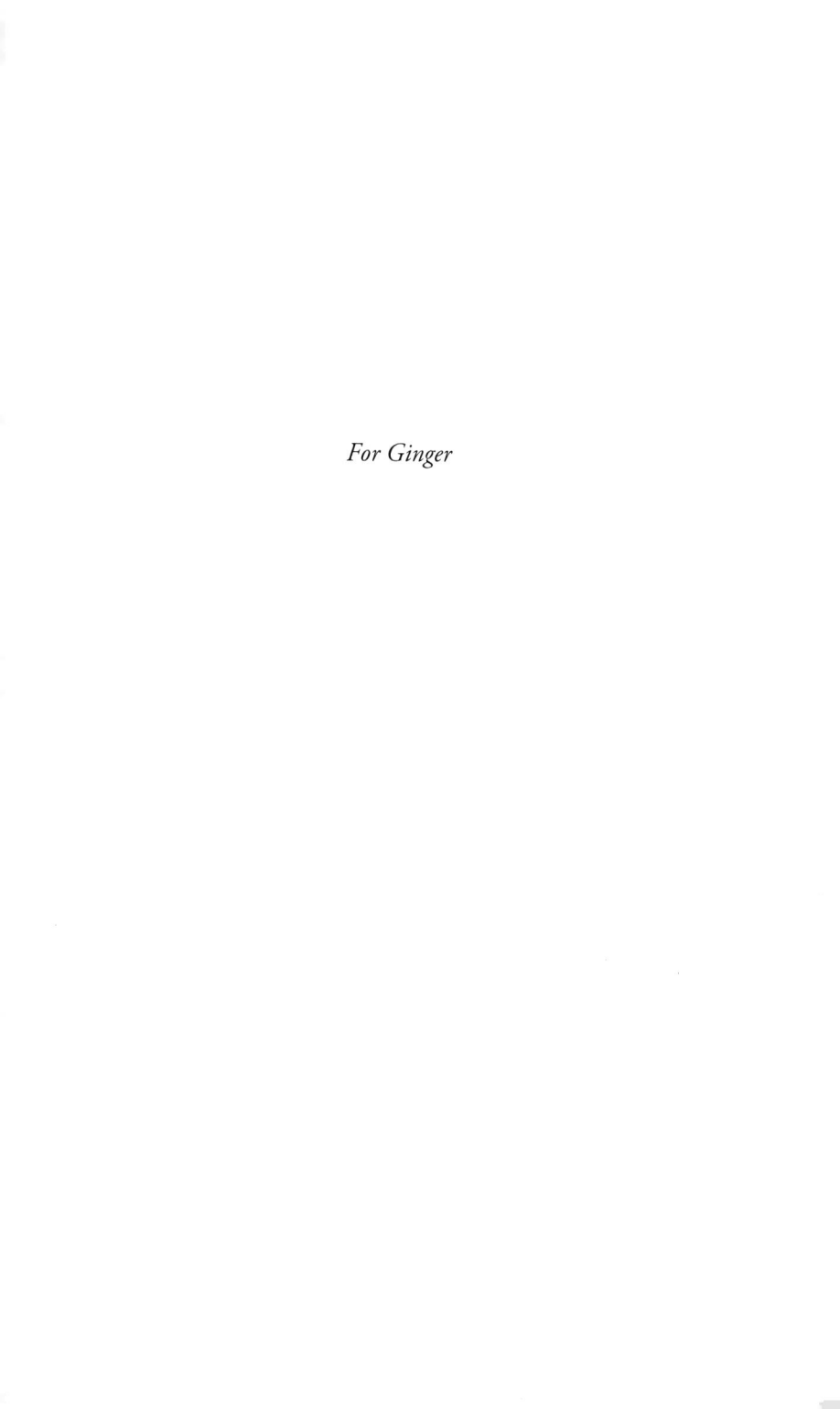

# CHAPTER 1

## Vanessa

In a small office, there was a desk. On the desk sat a glass model of a castle. Behind the desk sat an interviewer who had one final question for Vanessa.

"Is there anything else you'd like to share with us about your work history?"

A fine sweat threatened to mar her neat application of makeup.

"No, sir. I think we covered everything." Her crisp diction slipped on the last word and slid into the slightest hint of a Southern accent.

"Very well, then." The interviewer shuffled a few papers on his desk. "Would you mind stepping into the waiting room?"

"Of course." She tucked a wayward curl behind her ear as she reached for her bag, then stood up straight in her sensible heels, and walked with a steady tread to the door.

*Damn it all, woman, don't trip now.*

Out the office door she went, shutting it carefully behind her.

In the waiting room, her gaze settled on the wall-mounted television as it played a promotional video on a continuous loop. She went back and forth between glancing at the screen and checking her suit jacket and skirt for nonexistent lint.

"The Destiny Corporation offers competitive salaries, generous health benefits, and the most unique work environment in the world. If your dream is to make dreams come true, you'll feel right at home..."

One corner of her mouth lifted just a little. *You can make my dream come true by hiring me.*

"Vanessa?" The interviewer leaned out of his doorway and beckoned to her with a manila file folder. "Come on in."

She stood up and smoothed her jacket as best she could.

---

The interviewer folded his hands on the desk. "Thank you for taking the time to talk to me today. We've been looking for just the right person to take this role, and after speaking with you, we feel that you're up to the job. We'd like to offer you the position of area manager at Destiny Park."

Vanessa smiled. "That's wonderful," she said. "When do I start?"

"Right now."

Vanessa tried not to look shocked. Was this the usual procedure?

"I'm going to send you over to your office in the Legacy area of Destiny Park. Have you been to the park before?" He looked at her expectantly.

"It's been a while, but we went there on family vacations a couple of times when I was a kid. The Legacy area, you said?"

"Just call it 'Legacy' for short," he said. "Legacy, Fantasy, Galaxy, Discovery. The four themed lands of Destiny Park."

"Legacy, Fantasy, Galaxy, Discovery," she repeated dutifully. "Got it."

"You'll meet your staff first, then we'll arrange for you to introduce yourself to your employees later today, at the shift change. I know it's a bit sudden, but we're anxious to have someone in place as soon as possible. Does that work for you?"

"Of course." *What can I say? No? Hardly.*

"Great! Here are the directions to the manager parking lot, and a temporary badge to get you through the security gate." His handshake conveyed both congratulation and dismissal.

---

Vanessa hurried across the parking lot, eager to get to Destiny Park. As she pulled open the driver's side door of her car, she spotted movement out of the corner of her eye.

A turtle wobbled its way down from a nearby curb into the gutter of the busy road, intent on dodging cars.

Vanessa looked from the temporary badge in her hand to the turtle and back again, before huffing a sigh and jogging as quickly as she could manage in high heels across the parking lot.

She attempted to scoot the turtle back onto the curb with her foot. "Bad turtle," she said. "Stop that."

The turtle ignored her and continued to hurl itself down the curb and into the road.

Vanessa let loose a cry of frustration and hustled back to her car. She flung open the passenger side door, tossed down the badge, and snatched up a single sheet of folded newspaper. She unfolded it and took one last look at the headline: "Historic Family-Run Amusement Park to Close Permanently."

With a life at stake, there was no time to be sentimental.

She carried the paper to the curb and knelt next to the turtle.

With her hands protected by the newspaper, she lifted the turtle and carried it to a row of bushes far from the road. "Listen, you," she said as she deposited it behind a bush, "I might not be here next time to save your shell. So be a good turtle and stay away from the scary road, okay?"

Vanessa walked back to her car and slid into the driver's seat. *Good luck, turtle.*

---

The directions led to a broad highway flanked by pine forest. At the security gate, delicate, sparkling turrets were just visible above the trees.

Vanessa cranked her window down and passed the guard her temporary badge.

He studied it, then leaned down to her window.

"Do you know where you're going, ma'am?"

"Manager parking. I'm a manager," she said. *I'm a manager at Destiny Park!* She could hardly believe it.

The guard nodded. "Turn right past the lamppost. Wait till I lower the blockade first."

Vanessa thanked him and rolled up her window.

She looked ahead to the sturdy metal barrier painted in yellow and black. The barrier looked like jaws as it retracted into the ground, allowing her to drive over it and beyond.

She glanced in her rearview mirror as the barrier rose into position again.

The next turn took her through a tall earthen berm before revealing an open parking lot tucked behind several large buildings. The loose gravel on the ground made for an unsteady walk to the doorway marked "Crew Entrance."

Vanessa pushed open one of the heavy doors into a stairwell lit with buzzing fluorescent lights. As she descended, she realized that the offices must be located underneath the park, while the park itself occupied the second floor. The stairs switched back at a lower landing, then led directly into an underground corridor which stretched a long distance to the left and right. The awareness of an entire theme park over her head set off a shiver of claustrophobia.

Vanessa spotted a sign facing the stairs.

← Fantasy
← Galaxy
← Discovery
Legacy →

She headed up the corridor. Although she had been to Destiny Park a few times as a child, it was difficult to conjure any childhood memory well enough to navigate the theme park underground with no landmarks in sight.

The signs would have to do.

By the time she hiked to the correct office, she regretted wearing heels.

The plastic letters on the sign next to the door read "Legacy Management." Vanessa risked a quick peek through the narrow window.

Inside, a slender young woman sat at a desk near the door, pencil in hand, intent on a large notebook with a spiral binding at the top. She had round glasses and a thick cascade of dark brown braids spilling onto the shoulders of her pearl-buttoned white cardigan.

Vanessa drew back from the window and knocked on the door.

"It's open." The woman remained seated at her desk but flipped the cover of her notebook closed and slid it out of sight.

Vanessa opened the door and stepped into the office. "Hi, I'm Vanessa Jones. I'm the new manager for this area."

"Oh." The woman stared at Vanessa with expressive brown eyes. "I'm Charlotte, the secretary for Legacy."

"It's nice to meet you, Charlotte. Did the head office let you know I was coming?"

"Oh, yes." Charlotte started, as if recalling something, then yanked open one of her desk drawers and rummaged through it with great gusto. "This came for you." She stood up, revealing her willowy height, and handed a single sheet of paper across the desk to Vanessa.

Vanessa took it.

> *Vanessa Jones*
> *Legacy Management*
> *Destiny Park*
>
> *Dear Ms. Jones,*
>
> *Welcome to the management team of Destiny Park. You are scheduled to introduce yourself to the Legacy crew members at 5:00 p.m. in the American Dream theater. Please take*

*this afternoon to prepare, and to orient yourself within your assigned area.*

*I trust that your secretary, Charlotte, will be of help to you during this transition.*

*Regards,*
*Mr. Destiny*

She flipped the paper over. There was nothing more to it. "Is this how Mr. Destiny usually communicates?"

"He doesn't come around much. Or call. Mostly we just get memos. Like that one." Charlotte indicated the paper in Vanessa's hand.

Vanessa raised one eyebrow as she studied the brief missive again. "I guess he prefers the written word."

Charlotte shrugged.

"Well." Vanessa clicked her heels, momentarily at a loss for words. "Why don't you show me around?"

Vanessa followed Charlotte out the door and into the corridor. This time, she noticed what sounded like a radio announcer coming over the loudspeakers placed periodically along the ceiling of the corridor. It didn't sound like any of the local radio shows she'd heard. She could only make out a few words, thanks to the mysterious whooshing noises coming from the multicolored pipes in all sizes that ran along the corridor walls. "Parade... step off at... fireworks will illuminate... 10:00 p.m."

"Charlotte, what's that radio station?"

Charlotte glanced up at the nearest speaker. "That's our own radio station, The Voice of Destiny. It's broadcast underground so everyone can hear today's operating hours, parade schedule, and so on. Plus some pop music." As she talked, she kept a brisk pace in her flat-soled shoes.

Farther along, Vanessa spotted a Legacy sign with the arrow pointing up. She followed Charlotte into the stairwell.

They headed toward the sunlight streaming from a window on the upper landing.

Upon emerging, they stood together under a grand oak tree in the central plaza of Legacy.

"Over there, that's the American Dream theater." Charlotte gestured with her whole hand to an imposing building with columns in the Classical Revival style. "And over there, that's the Ghost Factory. The haunted house, you know?" She looked at Vanessa.

"Right," said Vanessa. "The haunted house."

Spiked iron gates surrounded a forbidding red brick factory facade.

Charlotte continued. "If you keep going that way, you get to the Gold Rush ride. It's a roller coaster. You've been here before, right?"

"Ages ago." Vanessa turned in a circle to get her bearings. "Have you worked here long?"

Charlotte removed her glasses and polished them on the corner of her sweater. "A few years, give or take. Long enough to see a few managers come and go."

*Is that a warning? I hope it's a friendly one.* "That's a good long time. You must know a lot about the park," Vanessa said. "Can we take a look inside the theater before we head back?"

They slipped in through a back entrance.

The theater contained several hundred empty seats facing a stage hung with thick velvet curtains bordered with gold fringe. Columns lit with dim spotlights lined the walls.

"There's a few minutes till the next show," Charlotte said, "but you can't go on the stage anyway, what with all the machinery up there. You'll just stand down front and talk."

Vanessa imagined the seats filled with her employees. Her heartbeat quickened as she paced the area between the stage and the first row of seats. She stopped and took a deep breath.

*This is it.*

"Let's go before they let the next group in," she said.

Vanessa glanced over her shoulder one last time before they exited the back way, just as the main entrance doors swung open without a sound.

Across the empty theater, a dark-haired man dressed in a colonial costume silently watched them leave.

## Thomas

Thomas flipped the switch that opened the theater doors. As they swung open, he spotted two figures walking to the back entrance of the theater.

*Charlotte? What's she doing here?* By the time he threaded his way to the front of the theater, they were gone. He opened the microphone box with a practiced flip of his hand and retrieved the handheld microphone. "Please move all the way to the center of the row to make room for others. Thank you." *Wonder who that was with her. Maybe they found another manager to replace the last disaster.*

Thomas delivered the rest of the pre-show spiel, pushed the button to start the show, and sat down in an empty theater seat. Patriotic music thrummed and robots gesticulated onstage, but Thomas might as well have been sitting in a Zen garden for all the notice he took.

*She was wearing a business suit; only managers wear those. The rest of us get to play dress up.* With that thought, he reached for his cravat and attempted to tug it into the proper shape. It was hopeless. There was too much humidity for it to do anything other than collapse.

A shaft of light beamed into the theater, then disappeared. Someone had opened and closed one of the entry doors. Thomas glanced over his shoulder into the dark. Only a fellow employee would know the layout well enough to stride into the dimly lit theater.

Thomas hopped up and met Charlotte halfway.

"They got a new one already," Charlotte said without preamble. "She's coming up to introduce herself at the shift change."

*Just what I need: another unknown.*

"What's she like?" he asked.

She tossed her hands up in the air. "How should I know? I got the memo from Mr. Destiny, she walked in the door, and here we are."

Thomas rubbed his forehead, speaking to himself almost as much as to her. "We're getting so close and they know it. That's why they didn't wait."

"Probably. Anyway, I gotta get back." She struck him on the arm playfully. "Don't worry." She turned to walk up the aisle.

Thomas rolled his eyes. He raised his voice so she could hear him over the show even as she walked away. "Right, I won't worry at all," he said. "Whatever was I thinking?"

The visitors near him stared. He bowed at them with a theatrical flourish before he returned to his seat. *It's all just part of the show.*

## CHAPTER 2

*Vanessa*

Charlotte leaned into Vanessa's office doorway, flapping a piece of paper in rhythmic waves through the air. "Looks like you got another memo."

Vanessa stood up from her desk, where she had been making notes for her speech, and stepped into the common area of the office. *I'll take any excuse to get out of that windowless box.* "Thanks, Charlotte." She took the paper and read it as Charlotte returned to her desk. "Wait—do you know anything about this?"

Vanessa read the memo aloud.

> *Vanessa Jones*
> *Legacy Management*
> *Destiny Park*
>
> *Dear Ms. Jones,*

*In order to provide additional support to you during this time of transition, one of our management interns has been reassigned to your area. He is scheduled to join you in your office shortly to become acquainted with you before the meeting.*

*Regards,*
*Mr. Destiny*

Before Charlotte could speak, someone knocked on the door. Vanessa and Charlotte looked at each other, looked at the door, and simultaneously called, "Come in!"

The office door opened to reveal a man about Charlotte's age who proceeded to ignore Charlotte and address Vanessa. "You must be the new Legacy manager. I'm Dirk." He nodded his head sharply, but his gelled blond hair didn't budge.

"I'm Vanessa." She shook hands with him, then introduced Charlotte. "This is the Legacy office secretary, Charlotte."

Charlotte offered Dirk a half-smile that appeared to cost her a great deal of effort.

He barely glanced at Charlotte before continuing to speak to Vanessa.

"I was the management intern over in Fantasy, but Mr. Destiny thought you could use an extra hand around here. You introducing yourself to the team today?" He put his hands in his khaki pants pockets and looked remarkably sure of himself, for an intern.

"In about an hour. Have you worked here long, Dirk?"

"Oh, yes. Quite a few years now. I waited a long time for an intern position to open up." Dirk's eyes were the same blue color as his long-sleeved dress shirt, and his gaze met hers with calculating coolness.

*And now you're waiting for a management position to open up. Swell.*

"That's wonderful," she said. "I'm so glad to have you join us."

Charlotte made a strangled sound that turned into a cough.

Vanessa glanced at Charlotte and continued. "However, I really must leave you to your own devices while I finish getting ready for the meeting. Charlotte, can you help me with something?" She went in her office.

Charlotte followed her and closed the door.

Both women remained standing, facing each other across the desk.

"What was that all about?" Vanessa asked.

"What was what about?" Charlotte looked far more amused than intimidated.

*For heaven's sake, I don't have time for this.* Already, she'd endured a job interview, rescued a turtle, gone down a rabbit hole into a strange underground world where she'd received not one but two odd messages from her new boss, and been saddled with an intern waiting in the wings for an open management position.

"Charlotte, I may be new here, but I wasn't born yesterday. Obviously, you know this guy. Obviously, you're less than thrilled he's here. You nearly laughed in his face when I said I was glad to have him. What's the deal?"

"You really want to know?" Charlotte asked.

"Yes, please. Have a seat and tell me all about it." She gestured with an open hand, just like she'd seen Charlotte gesture earlier.

Thus encouraged, Charlotte practically skipped into a chair, then scooted it closer to Vanessa's desk with the air of someone bursting to share a secret.

Vanessa exhaled and sat down. *Thank goodness.*

"His name is Dirk. Also known as Dirk the Jerk," said Charlotte.

Vanessa raised her eyebrows. "Dirk the Jerk? Are you serious?"

Charlotte was just getting warmed up. "He's worked everywhere at Destiny. Upper management loves him because he'll do anything if he thinks it will benefit him." She made a face of distaste. "But he's never gotten a manager job because they don't really view him as management material. He's bounced from Fantasy to Galaxy to Discovery to here. I'm sure he thinks he's on his way up, but that's just because he's an arrogant…" She trailed off with a smile.

"Yes, I see what you mean." Vanessa tried to hide her own smile and failed spectacularly. "Bless their managerial hearts. I can see why they like him so much."

---

The American Dream theater filled up as crew members came off their shifts on the Legacy attractions Gold Rush and Ghost Factory. Gold miners in wide-brimmed hats and scarlet neckerchiefs mixed with factory workers in Victorian garb. A handful of men and women in colonial costume closed down the theater for the day, then took their seats.

Vanessa noticed one man who, unlike the teens and twenty-somethings, was approximately her age. He sprawled into his seat and stretched out like a louche aristocrat. He ran long fingers through waves of black hair. It was almost distracting. She shifted her gaze away after holding it there for one beat too long.

Vanessa waited for everyone to settle, then walked to the center of the space in front of the stage.

"Good afternoon." Vanessa took a slow breath in and out before continuing. "Thank you for coming today. My name is Vanessa Jones, and I am the new manager for the Legacy area. You already know Charlotte, our area secretary." She gestured to Charlotte, who gave a little wave.

Many of the crew waved back.

"And this is Dirk, who is joining us from Fantasy as our management intern." She turned to Dirk, who clenched both hands above his head like he was being cheered by fans, except he wasn't.

She turned to face the audience again. "I don't want you to feel like I'm a stranger, so here's a little about me," she said. "I'm new to Florida but not new to theme parks. I started working at an amusement park in my hometown when I was just 19. I worked my way up, became a manager, and I helped manage the place until it closed down last year. I'm thrilled to be at Destiny Park and I can't wait to get to know all of you. I don't want to keep you long," she added, "but if you have any questions I can answer, I'll be happy to do so."

Several hands shot up.

"Yes, young lady in the Gold Rush costume?" Vanessa pointed to a woman in the fifth row.

"Have you heard anything about a raise?"

"Well, I just got here, so I haven't heard anything yet, but I'll check on it."

A man wearing a Victorian vest and dress shirt with striped slacks raised his hand.

"Yes?" said Vanessa.

"Are you aware of the overtime issue?"

*Sounds like there are several ongoing issues here.* "Not yet, but I will catch up on that as soon as possible."

They forgot to raise their hands and called out one after another.

"Is someone going to do something about the unsafe costume pieces?"

"Why are our hours getting cut back again?"

The dark-haired man Vanessa noticed earlier raised his hand. She called on him. "Yes?"

He swept his hair back with one hand as he stood up, his height lending an air of grace to his figure.

The crowd quieted.

A faint smile played around his lips before he spoke. "Which attraction are you training on first?"

Yet another question for which she didn't have an immediate answer. Vanessa stalled for time. "I'm sorry, what was your name?"

"Thomas."

"Thomas, I'm not sure I know what you're referring to." She glanced at Charlotte in an attempt to pick up some sort of cue.

Charlotte didn't notice.

"New managers have to get trained on all their attractions. Which one are you doing first?" His voice, low yet resonant, easily carried across the theater.

Determined not to be at a loss for at least one question, she picked one of the three attractions at random. "American Dream," she said. *Seems appropriate.*

He smiled. "I look forward to it," he said, inclining his head in an almost courtly fashion.

## Thomas

Thomas sat down. *Does she realize what she's gotten into yet? If not, she soon will. I almost feel sorry for her.* He observed her as she wrapped up the meeting. She had a centeredness about her that created its own gravity.

When the meeting concluded, Thomas leapt out of his seat and hurried to the front of the theater. "Charlotte! Do you have the new training roster for me yet?"

"I will as soon as I get with Vanessa." Charlotte turned to Vanessa. "Vanessa, Thomas is the trainer for the Legacy area. He teaches new crew members how to run the attractions in our area."

Vanessa addressed Thomas. "So that's why you asked me that question instead of quizzing me on the issue of the day."

Dirk interrupted. "They're like children demanding dessert, aren't they?"

Thomas, who up to that moment had been on the receiving end of Vanessa's attention, slowly turned his head to Dirk. "Dirk. I hadn't heard you were coming to Legacy. What happened in Fantasy? Did they finally learn everything you had to impart?" *You idiot.*

Dirk replied as if Thomas were serious. "Oh, yes, Mr. Destiny"—he dropped the name with relish—"felt it was time for a lateral move."

"Really," Thomas replied flatly.

Charlotte, after watching the exchange like a cat at a tennis match, turned to Vanessa. "You ready?"

"I sure am. Nice to meet you, Thomas."

"Likewise."

Thomas leaned against the stage and watched them walk away.

After the theater emptied, he headed underground to change out of his costume. Street clothes were more comfortable than the George Washington getup he wore when he worked American Dream, but he had to admit that the colonists exhibited a certain sense of style that was missing in modern t-shirts and jeans. He tossed the costume into a large laundry bin on his way out of the locker room.

One of the perks of working at Destiny Park was the ability to visit the park after your shift. Thomas followed the underground corridor to the nearest stairwell and took the stairs two at a time to the park above, emerging in the Fantasy area. The sun blazed like it would be summer forever, but a cool breeze hinted at the season to come.

Thomas entered the Fantasy bazaar. The scent of melted caramel beckoned him to a concession stand, where he purchased a waxed paper bag of caramel corn. Holding the warm bag safely in one hand, he slid through the bustling crowd like a ghost to emerge on the other side of the bazaar. He took a seat on a bench facing a small stage topped with a wooden awning, then contentedly popped a piece of sweet caramel corn into his mouth.

A stirring musical theme poured from the speakers. Two dancers, one man and one woman, circled each other, striking poses that highlighted their differences, swirling together then apart, tracing an invisible spiral that compelled them to meet in the center of the stage. They struck a final pose face to face, a secret smile on his lips and a sparkle in her eyes, as if there were no audience to observe them. After holding the pose, they recovered and bowed before walking gracefully offstage.

He always enjoyed watching these dancers. To see them, and to indulge in his favorite snack, had become a weekly pastime. For some reason, today's performance left him with a slight ache in his chest. There were other acts to follow, but Thomas had seen what he had come to see. He folded up his empty bag, dropped it into one of the ubiquitous trash cans, and disappeared into the crowd.

## CHAPTER 3

*Vanessa*

The calico gown wasn't a problem, but no matter how many times she attempted to stuff her hair into the puffy white cap, messy tendrils popped out along the edges.

"I feel ridiculous," Vanessa said, rotating slowly in front of a large mirror in the underground costume department.

*There goes my authority.* She stood in front of the mirror and tried to cram her hair securely into the cap one more time. It was no use. *One look at me in this outfit and they'll all be in stitches.* She tugged the edges of the neckline to make sure they covered her bra straps. *Who on God's green earth decided that dressing up managers for training would be a good idea?*

Having brought a pink flush to her cheeks, she flounced out and went to the office.

Charlotte looked up from her work as Vanessa came in. Her gaze traveled all the way down to the hemline of the dress, then back up until she reached the frilly cap. "Oh, wow," she said. She attempted to rally. "You look…"

"Don't say it," Vanessa said.

"No, really—"

"Like an off-brand Martha Washington?" Vanessa finished.

Charlotte laughed. "Like you work here. I mean, I know you work here, but now you look like a crew member. You could pass."

"Then I'll fit right in. Where's Thomas?" Vanessa adjusted her cap again.

"He should be here soon."

"What about Dirk?" asked Vanessa.

"He went to handle something upstairs," said Charlotte.

"And what are you up to today?"

Charlotte rifled through the papers on her desk. "I got some scheduling, some shift changes, a few reports to send to the head office. The usual. Why? You need something?"

Vanessa tried to scratch an impossible-to-reach spot on her shoulder blade. *What do they make this fabric out of? Asbestos?* "Yes, I wanted to follow up on the questions everyone was asking at the meeting, but it'll have to wait till later." By contorting herself she managed to reach the spot and set about scratching it industriously.

The office door opened. Thomas, wearing a colonial gentleman's costume, took in her attire at a glance. "My lady! Are you ready?"

"I was born ready," said Vanessa, recovering her dignity and shaking out her skirt. "Let's go."

---

"Have you seen the show before?" Thomas asked as they went through a turnstile surrounded by a polished brass enclosure.

"Years ago, when I was a kid. I don't really remember it."

They entered the circular lobby of the American Dream theater. Red, white, and blue bunting draped every lintel and column. Sculptures symbolizing the achievements of industrialists and explorers sat under spotlights. A crowd milled around, waiting for the next show and ignoring the copies of presidential portraits hung next to oversized display cases filled with the dresses of former First Ladies.

Thomas showed her the lobby microphone hidden inside a wall-mounted box. He opened a side door and let her peek into a break room just off the lobby.

One of the crew members on break dug into a container of yogurt while another sported a large set of headphones over her white cap.

Vanessa waved, then retreated into the lobby.

Thomas made the showtime announcement over the lobby microphone, then showed Vanessa how to push the button to open the automatic doors. The crowd poured into the theater and Thomas stationed himself at the theater control box, which contained a microphone and the button that started the show. Vanessa took up a position next to him.

"Please move all the way to the center of the row and fill in all available spaces. Thank you," he said.

*He has a nice voice.*

Thomas finished off the introduction spiel and hung up the microphone.

Vanessa pushed the button to start the show. They sat down next to each other in the rapidly dimming theater.

## Thomas

Thomas glanced at Vanessa out of the corner of his eye. Her hair was falling out of the cap again. He resisted an inexplicable urge to tuck it back in.

*She has pretty hair.*

He turned his attention to the show, which he had watched a thousand times. He could have recited the whole thing aloud, and had done so, on occasion, as a party trick. He wondered if it would amuse his new boss. She appeared to be watching the show with interest as it presented a condensed version of selected events in American history.

As the triumphant closing theme blared, Thomas beckoned to Vanessa. They resumed their positions next to the control box. Thomas delivered the parting words and opened the exit doors with a touch of a button.

The crowd ambled into the glare of the morning light.

When the last visitor had left, Thomas indicated the door controls to Vanessa, who closed the doors and dusted her hands with satisfaction.

"What's next?" she said.

"This time, you do the talking," Thomas replied. "I'll get you a copy of the spiel."

"Please move all the way to the center of the row?" she said.

"That's the spirit," Thomas said.

They walked back to the lobby. Script in hand, Vanessa handled all the microphone and button duties for the next show with aplomb. By the time the show had finished for the second time, it was almost lunchtime.

"Are you ready for lunch?" asked Thomas.

Vanessa patted her stomach. "I could be. You?"

"Most definitely. Did you know the summer crew festival is today? They're giving out free ice cream and watermelon in the manager parking lot."

"So that's why I had trouble finding a parking spot this morning. Free ice cream for everyone? That's pretty nice."

"Almost as nice as a wage that actually pays the bills," Thomas said, and immediately regretted it.

*I shouldn't have said that. I am an idiot.*

Had he made her uncomfortable? He could have kicked himself. No matter how friendly his boss was, it didn't excuse letting down his guard in her presence. "I'm sorry. It's all any of the crew are talking about these days. It rubs off on you."

"Man cannot live by ice cream alone," she said.

Thomas couldn't help laughing. "Maybe if it was rocky road?"

They made their way to the manager parking lot and approached the temporary white tent erected off to the side.

"I should have asked—did you want to start with a sandwich or something?" said Thomas.

"No," said Vanessa. "We're adults—we can give ourselves permission to have ice cream for lunch." She ordered double scoops of strawberry and vanilla.

"I knew I liked you," said Thomas. He ordered scoops of chocolate, vanilla, and strawberry in a bowl.

They looked around for a place to sit. When they found all the seats taken, Vanessa suggested they sit in her car. She unlocked the driver's side door and leaned across, ice cream tipping precariously, to unlock the passenger side door.

"Nice car," said Thomas as he sat down. He pulled the lever to recline the seat.

"Thanks," she said. "It's a little small, but I like it."

"Call it snug," said Thomas. "Or cozy." He scooped a bit of vanilla and chocolate together.

Vanessa swirled the ice cream around in her bowl. "You know, this isn't what I was expecting when I moved down here."

"No?"

"It's different. So much money went into making this place beautiful. Not that my old park wasn't nice," she said. "It was just—how do I put this—simpler? Homegrown?"

"Was that better?" Thomas asked.

"I don't know," she said. "I feel a little like the country mouse in the city."

"Maybe that's a good thing. It's a fresh perspective."

She nodded, appearing to consider his words. "I hope you're right."

They finished up their ice cream lunch.

After Vanessa locked the car doors, she turned to Thomas. "What's next? Oh, wait—you have something there. Right there." She pointed at his face.

Thomas groped his face all over, feeling for melted ice cream. "Where?" Embarrassment curled around the ice cream in his belly.

"No, not there. There," she said.

He patted his face faster, finding nothing.

"May I?" she asked.

He sighed and nodded.

She held her hand lightly along his jawline and rubbed her thumb across his jaw. "There. All clear."

"Thank you. We can go get changed now," he said, gesturing for her to go first.

As he followed her down the stairs, his hand traced where hers had touched.

After picking up a fresh costume at the window for himself, and helping Vanessa select her items, he breezed into the locker room to change costumes for the next attraction.

Thomas rather liked the Gold Rush costume. It came with a broad-brimmed hat he could wear at a rakish angle. He didn't love the garish neckerchief, but acknowledged that it certainly fit the theme even if it wasn't the most attractive accessory. He observed himself in the mirror. *Pants zipped? Check. Shirt smoothly tucked in? Check. Hat at the right angle?* He made a slight adjustment. *Check.*

Outside the locker room he spotted Vanessa fully kitted out in brown slacks, a beige blouse, a red neckerchief, and the signature Gold Rush brown felt hat. "Have you been on the ride before?" he asked as they walked to Gold Rush.

"I'm not much of a roller coaster person," she said.

"No? Me neither. But," he clarified, "even I like Gold Rush. It's not too rough and the drops aren't too big." He led the way to an outdoor overlook where they could watch the ride in action. Each time a train swooped past their position, the happy screams of the riders faded in, increased to full volume, and faded out like someone had rapidly dialed a volume control up and down.

"Does it go upside down?" she asked.

"Nope."

She watched the ride for another minute. "I can handle it," she said.

"You sure?"

"Positive. Oh!" she said. She touched her hat. "Where can I stash this thing?"

He swept his hat off and held it out as if he were taking up a collection. "With mine."

She nested her hat neatly inside of his and followed him to the loading area, where he deposited their hats behind a podium. They stepped into one of the two-person cars and pulled down the lap bar.

The train ambled out of the station and climbed the first hill. Thomas eyed Vanessa. Her face was serene, but her hands gripped the lap bar. "Here we go!" he cheered as they reached the top. The train swept down the hill and around a corner past abandoned carts heaped with ore.

They couldn't help sliding from side to side and bumping into each other as the train careened along the track. When they swerved through a cave streaked with sparkling gold veins, Vanessa's head tipped back and she laughed in delight.

Thomas applauded as the train pulled into the station, leading the entire train full of visitors—and Vanessa—in an impromptu standing ovation as they exited.

"That was fun!" she exulted.

He smiled broadly and returned her hat, sweeping his hair back before putting on his own. "Now you get to see behind the scenes," he said.

The control tower contained an intimidating array of buttons that operated loading gates, ride vehicle doors, emergency brakes, and a PA system, not to mention an internal phone handset and a bank of old computer monitors displaying a constant cascade of system notifications. Thomas noticed Vanessa's forehead furrowing as her gaze traveled across the controls. "Don't worry," he reassured her. "You don't have to know all of this like a crew member would. That would take days. You're just here to get the basic idea."

They stood in the background as the control tower crew member deftly dispatched ride vehicles one after another in synchrony with the crew loading and unloading below.

"It's not that," she said, still focused on the controls. "I'm not worried. I'm just comparing your controls to the roller coaster I used to run."

Intrigued, he asked the crew member at the controls to stand aside. Thomas took the seat and gestured for Vanessa to come closer. He caught a faint scent of roses as she leaned over his shoulder. *Focus, Thomas.* He narrated his actions as he ran through the sequence of controls that operated the ride.

After watching the process through several arriving and departing trains, she recited the sequence without a flaw.

"Well done," he said with sincere admiration, ceding the controls back to the control tower crew member.

"All in a day's work," she replied, and tipped her hat.

## Vanessa

After she completed her Gold Rush training, they returned to the costume department to change into their normal attire.

*One more training day. Then everything will be back to normal.* She would be back in her regular clothes, back in her office, back to the familiar feeling of exercising a reasonable amount of authority. Being the supervisor, not the supervised.

Wearing a costume blurred the lines.

When she came out of the ladies' locker room, she felt unsure whether she should wait for Thomas or not. She decided it would be impolite to leave without saying goodbye, then wondered if perhaps he had already changed and left.

He hadn't. He strode through the swinging doors of the locker room and into the main hallway. "See you tomorrow," he said when he spotted her. She waved back and realized she hardly recognized him in street clothes. She wondered how he would look in the Ghost Factory costume.

When Vanessa entered the Legacy office, Charlotte glanced up. "You didn't want to be a lady gold miner for the rest of the day?"

"I'm not going to dignify that with an answer," said Vanessa.

"Suit yourself."

The door opened. Dirk carried a folded sheet of paper as he walked in. "I had to run an errand up to the head office, so I went ahead and picked this up for you while I was there. Thought I'd save someone a trip." He handed it to Vanessa.

*Did you read it already? Of course you did.*

She unfolded it.

*Vanessa Jones*
*Legacy Management*
*Destiny Park*

*Dear Ms. Jones,*

*Please join us in the head office at 5:00 p.m. today for an all-hands meeting.*

*Regards,*
*Mr. Destiny*

"Fine. Charlotte, I'm going upstairs for a management meeting. Dirk, you keep an eye on things here. I'll update you later."

Having gotten the hang of navigating the underground corridors, Vanessa emerged at the nexus of Legacy, Fantasy, Discovery, and Galaxy, into the center of Destiny Park informally known as the Hub.

The castle in the center of the plaza nearly blinded her. Sun reflected from vast panels of glass with a mirror-like finish. The Mirror Castle, as it was known, reflected vistas from all of the surrounding areas, as well as the daytime illumination. Although the glass was not entirely opaque, it was still impossible to see from the outside what the inside contained.

Narrow panes broke Vanessa's reflection into thin shards as she approached the hidden elevator to the head office. Vanessa stepped inside and pushed the button. When the doors opened again, she stepped out into a plain and narrow hallway with a low ceiling. The drabness of the castle interior contrasted sharply with its glossy exterior. She followed the sound of voices around a corner to find the meeting room.

A large oval table almost filled the room. She took a seat. No one sat in the chair at the head of the table. None of the managers present made any attempt at small talk.

*Tough crowd.*

It was against her nature not to greet those seated next to her, so she settled for a polite nod to the managers on her left and right in lieu of friendly conversation.

Mr. Destiny strode into the room. He pulled out the chair at the head of the table, whipped off his suit jacket, handed it to an aide, and sat down heavily in the chair. He leaned back, clasped both hands behind his bald head, and surveyed the assembled managers. "Thank you for coming. I know you are all anxious about our situation," he said, leaning forward and using his fingers to put air quotes around the word "situation."

Vanessa looked around the table. Other managers were nodding along, so she did her best to match their concerned expressions. It didn't seem like a good time to point out the fact that she had absolutely no idea what the "situation" was.

Mr. Destiny continued. "I think we're making headway with most of the crew. The summer festival, with the free ice cream and so on, I think that's showing people that we care." He spoke as if reciting an immutable scientific law. "They don't need to join a union when we have their best interests at heart."

*Oh, boy.* Everything fell into place at once. *The employees are trying to organize.*

*No wonder they were asking all those questions.*

*No wonder they were so eager to fill the job and get a manager in here. I bet they would have hired anyone who could fog a mirror, just to make sure they had someone in place.*

Mr. Destiny was still pontificating. "So I want you to keep on doing what you're doing. Keep talking about how they're free to join or not join. Keep talking about how much union dues take out of their hard-earned paychecks. Tell them to let you know if the union organizers are harassing them, so you can protect them. Besides," he said, making an exaggerated gesture to display his watch, "they have less than 30 days left until the election. We have the advantage here. No one likes change. No one likes somebody coming around harping on things and stirring up trouble. All you have to do, on the other hand, is present the facts and emphasize what a great place this is to work."

Vanessa wanted to sink into her chair.

*What have I gotten myself into?*

## CHAPTER 4

*Vanessa*

The next morning, the last thing in the world Vanessa wanted to do was dress up in yet another ridiculous costume.

Yet there she was, seated on a worn wooden bench in the ladies' locker room, attempting to tug a thick black stocking over her foot without twisting it upside down in the process. A long, dark green skirt went over the stockings. She stood up and tucked her white high-necked blouse into the skirt, then put an apron over the whole ensemble. Facing the mirror, she stuck a half-dozen bobby pins between her lips and gathered her hair into a pile on top of her head, pinning it down section by section.

When her hair was secure, she turned around slowly in front of the mirror.

*I look like a maid.*

The observation did not please her. At least the American Dream dress had been frilly enough to be somewhat charming. She missed the Gold Rush hat.

When she walked into the Legacy office, Dirk was pouring himself a cup of coffee. He looked up at her as she walked in. "Are you here to iron my shirts?" he said, clearly pleased with his joke.

She stared at him. *I'll iron the shirt you wear at your funeral.* "No, I'm going to train with Thomas this morning."

"Right. Well." He took a sip of coffee. "There's an update on the 'situation' this morning." He paused dramatically.

Vanessa waited for him to continue but refused to give him the satisfaction of a response.

"They want us to keep an eye on the organizers. Make sure they're not doing anything they're not supposed to. See if they're breaking any rules."

"Isn't that retaliation?" she asked.

"If you do it right, it's just good business practices." He leaned toward Vanessa and stage-whispered. "I already have a few people in mind."

"Do you, now?" Vanessa was starting to feel the need for a cup of coffee. Or three.

Then the door opened.

Thomas entered wearing tailored slacks, a starched white shirt, and a vest of some satiny material underneath an elegant knee-length coat with wide velvet lapels. Whereas Vanessa's Ghost Factory costume was modeled to look like a factory worker, his costume was styled to look like a factory owner.

"Good morning," he said.

*All he needs is a top hat. Would a cane be too much?*
She made a mental picture of the full ensemble.

"I already asked her to iron my shirts," said Dirk, who couldn't let a bad joke go unrepeated.

Thomas didn't even look at him. Instead, he addressed Vanessa. "Shall we?"

Vanessa, who had been utterly lost in thought, collected herself just in time to answer in the affirmative before leading the way out.

She came to an abrupt stop in the middle of the corridor as the door closed behind her. "I'm sorry, Thomas, I know we're on a schedule, but if I don't get a cup of coffee, I'm going to die."

He laughed. "You don't have to apologize to me. Do you want to go back to the office?"

A vehement "No!" escaped her before she could stop it. "I mean, isn't there somewhere else we can go?"

"What, you don't want the pleasure of Dirk the—" He cleared his throat before continuing, "Dirk's company?"

It would be too easy to give in and banter with Thomas. She had to remind herself to be diplomatic without breaking ranks. "I'd like to breathe some fresh air, to be honest."

Thomas led her upstairs and around a corner to a tiny backstage cafe. Coffee in hand, they returned underground to walk the distance across the park before emerging upstairs in a deserted alley next to the Ghost Factory ride.

Vanessa could hear the ride soundtrack faintly through the walls of the building. The orientation of the alley created a funnel effect, which kept a light breeze moving through the area.

Thomas gestured with the hand that held his coffee. "Fresh air, right?"

She faced into the breeze and let it push the loose tendrils of hair away from her face as she sipped her coffee. "Lovely."

He leaned against the building.

"Thomas, you've been here a while, right? Can I ask you something?"

"Shoot."

"We had a meeting yesterday about the Destiny Park employees who are trying to unionize." She paused, trying to choose the right words. "Can you fill me in, at all, on what's going on?" She watched his face closely while trying not to be too obvious about it. He appeared to be gathering his thoughts.

"What do you want to know?" He met her gaze. It felt strangely intense. She looked away and took a sip of her coffee.

"How do people feel about it?"

"People?" he asked.

"You know what I mean."

"Like, manager people? You're a manager, you should know what they think," said Thomas.

She gave him a look. "I'm not asking about managers."

Thomas exhaled slowly. "Why don't you ask Charlotte?"

"Charlotte works in an office. It's not the same," said Vanessa.

"True. The secretaries aren't organizing. Yet." He tipped back his coffee cup for the last drop. "You could ask me how I feel about it."

*I was, you infuriating man.* "How do you feel about it?"

"I'm not sure if I like talking politics," he said. He turned and tossed his cup into a nearby trash can. "Wouldn't you rather be a ghost in the factory?" He leaned against the wall and grinned at her.

"A haunting answer," she said.

*But not a real answer, and you know it.*

## Thomas

*She knows. She's on to me. My God, I'm actually sweating.* He touched the back of his neck lightly and came away with moisture on his fingertips. He turned his head to see her walking behind him, following him to Ghost Factory. He noticed that her eyes were green, but in doing so, failed to watch where he put his feet, then tripped on a cobblestone and fell over.

She was beside him in an instant, one hand under his forearm and another behind his shoulder, stabilizing him as best she could.

Thomas colored. *If I'm going to get fired for union organizing, it'd be nice if I didn't fall on my face first.*

"Are you all right?" Her eyes were kind and filled with concern.

Thomas nodded and got to his feet. *If I get fired by her, it will be like being murdered by an angel.* He shook his head to try to clear it. "Never better!"

He thought fast. "Why don't we go on a ride-through first? I can recover, and you can see the ride from a visitor's point of view before we get into the technical side of things."

He took a shortcut to the loading area through a side door. They stepped onto a moving walkway lit with simulated gas lamps, then into a ride vehicle resembling a small open carriage.

As the carriage moved forward into the darkness, Thomas tried to impose logic on the thoughts tumbling through his mind. *I am a crew member trying to start a union in a hostile environment. She is a manager.*

*She is my natural enemy.*

Just as that thought passed through his head, his natural enemy happily exclaimed at a life-size ghost horse appearing to draw the carriage forward.

Thomas squeezed his eyes closed. The soundtrack, so faint from outside the building, was deafening within it. He felt a headache coming on.

They proceeded through one show scene after another. Vanessa attended to it all with apparent pleasure while Thomas, normally immune to every phantasmagorical effect, fervently wished it would all just go away.

It was the longest ride he'd ever been on.

Afterward, he escorted her to a tiny triangular break room wedged into a corner of the attraction building.

The crew members in the break room became noticeably uncomfortable in the presence of the almighty area manager, so Thomas and Vanessa didn't linger long before they slipped back through the velvet curtain and into the public area of the attraction. Thomas wondered, with some relief, how she would manage to get any intelligence on what was happening if all the crew simply clammed up around her.

They spent the rest of the morning practicing each station in the attraction. His favorite duty by far was to entertain the visitors entering the building. Thomas whipped open the attraction entrance door from the inside, startling the visitors closest to the entryway. "All right, you lot, any person coming in late shall pay a fine. Step lively, that's the way!" The first visitors in line hesitantly stepped over the threshold. "I hope you washed yourselves today?"

Someone in the crowd laughed and shouted back, "Not me!"

"Insolent language and oaths will not be tolerated," Thomas fired back, fully in character as a Victorian factory overseer. "In you go, ladies and gents." He motioned the visitors into the first room of the attraction. "Keep in mind that any person leaving his or her station or talking with other workers will be dismissed. Drop waste on the floor and you shall be fined. Got it, lad?" He glared at a young boy holding a lollipop with a dangling wrapper.

The boy giggled and stuck his tongue out.

Thomas made his way through the crowd to trigger the door to the next waiting area. "Remember, you are required to give four weeks notice if you wish to leave, but we may dismiss you at any time without notice."

The door to the loading area slid open, but none of the visitors moved. "Don't just stand there," he chided. "The devil makes work for idle hands."

When the last of the group of visitors had straggled through the door to the loading area, Thomas closed it and returned to the exterior door to repeat the process.

This time when he opened the door, he opened it to a little girl in the front, who appeared to be on the verge of tears.

Dropping his Ghost Factory persona, he immediately kneeled to her level and spoke in a gentle tone. "What's wrong, princess?"

She peered around him to the dark interior of the attraction. "I'm scared the ghosts will get me."

"Oh, no," Thomas said, very seriously. "We don't have that kind of ghost here. Only silly ghosts. Are you afraid of silly ghosts?"

She shook her head solemnly.

"Well, then." Thomas smiled at her. "You have nothing to worry about. Would you like to be my helper and let the people into the ride?"

Her eyes brightened. "All right," she said.

They walked side by side into the first room, the girl's family right behind them with the rest of the crowd following.

"You know how to say 'Open sesame,' don't you?" said Thomas.

The girl opened her mouth as if to say it right then and there.

"Not yet—it's very powerful, you know. Only to be used when absolutely necessary. Now, face this door."

She faced the door with an air of great concentration.

"Ready?" He secretly positioned his hand over the button that triggered the door. "Now!"

"Open sesame!" said the girl.

The door slid open as if by magic. Thomas applauded. The girl marched into the loading area with a big smile on her face. Thomas caught Vanessa's eye and winked.

After they'd worked their way through the rest of the stations, they returned for lunch to the little cafe where they'd picked up coffee earlier in the day. They sat at a rickety outdoor table and dined companionably on premade sandwiches and iced tea.

"So, I noticed you have a little accent... is that a Southern thing you have going on?" Thomas asked in between bites.

Vanessa cocked her head and looked quite serious. "Is it that obvious?"

"No! Not at all. I mean," he fumbled for the right words, "don't get me wrong."

Her serious expression disappeared and her eyes twinkled. "I'm just messing with you. I know it's obvious. I try to keep the 'y'alls' in check most of the time."

Thomas chuckled. "I know what you mean. I have a tendency to talk like I'm onstage even when I'm not. Old habits die hard."

"What did you do before you started working here?" she asked.

"You want my life story?"

"Give me the highlights," said Vanessa, settling back with her iced tea in hand.

"Let's see. I'm a local boy—can you believe it?"

She shook her head. "Seems like everybody here is from somewhere else. You must be the exception," she said.

"Exactly. Went to high school in a Podunk town on the coast I bet you've never heard of. Dropped out of college, went to New York, tried to make it as an actor... did not make it as an actor," he finished. "Came back here and got a job at Destiny because they were hiring and I like to eat."

"Don't we all," she drawled.

"What about you?"

"Me?" Vanessa gathered up her sandwich wrapper. "What's to know?" She pushed back her chair and looked at her watch. "I sprang fully formed from the sea." She winked at him.

"Don't try to scare me off with mythological references," he said.

She laughed. "I promise I'll fill you in another time." She stood up and looked down at him. "It's been fun. Thank you."

He didn't want lunch to be over. He rose from his chair anyway. "You're welcome."

He watched her walk away, her green skirt rippling in the wind.

As she walked, she pulled the pins out of her hair one at a time.

# CHAPTER 5

## Vanessa

Vanessa settled into her chair. A full day stretched before her with no trainings and no costumes. She felt she'd earned a quiet morning to sip a cup of coffee and catch up on paperwork. She set her coffee within reach and laid out her papers with enough space to identify them and be able to flip pages as needed. Her pens and pencils lay in a row.

Everything was in order.

She sighed happily.

She'd picked up the first paper in the stack when someone knocked at the door. "Come in," she called.

Dirk walked in, closed the door behind him, and sat down without being invited to have a seat.

*So much for a relaxing morning of coffee and paperwork.*

"Please, have a seat," she said, putting down the paper in her hand. "Can I help you with something?"

"I thought you might like to make a plan for dealing with this union thing. You know, putting pressure on the ringleaders? Getting the crew on our side?"

"We're not on the same side as our crew?" She knew what his answer would be, but wanted to hear him flounder his way into it.

"Of course we're on their side, if they're on the company's side," he said.

She regarded him from across the desk. She hadn't met anyone at Destiny Park whom she liked less than Dirk, but that didn't mean he couldn't be useful, perhaps in ways he didn't anticipate. "I'm listening," she said.

He took the cue. "First, we know some of the Legacy crew must be involved in convincing people to join the union. Otherwise, there wouldn't be enough support for it to even get off the ground."

"True. Go on."

"By that rationale, whoever is involved can't just be hiding out and biding their time. The only way to convince people to vote for the union is to actually go out and convince people. That's where these 'organizers' reveal themselves," he said. "All we have to do is see who's instigating the conversations."

"Then what?"

Dirk gave her a knowing look, like a second-rate mafioso. "We do what we have to do."

"I see," she said. "How do you propose we get that information? I walked into the Ghost Factory break room yesterday and everyone clammed up."

He looked smug. "Of course, you haven't been here long," he said. "But I have. I know some people I can talk to."

She resisted the impulse to throw her coffee mug at him, scalding hot coffee included.

"I appreciate that suggestion," she said, "but what about the part where we get people on our side?"

He rubbed his hands together before he continued. "Simple. Every time one of us goes on a walkthrough, or supervises the parade route, we have friendly little chats with the crew. Hit the talking points. Let them know they don't need a union to come between us and them."

Not only did he sound like a second-rate mafioso, he sounded like an ersatz Mr. Destiny. *He would probably take that as a compliment.*

He was watching her and waiting for her response.

*I need to stall for time.*

The whole situation made her uneasy, but she couldn't let him know that—and she wasn't even sure how to balance appeasing Mr. Destiny with respecting her employees' rights. For now, she had to feign agreement. "It could work. We only have—what is it now? Less than a month?"

"Less than a month," he confirmed.

"I want you to run up to the head office and see what you can find in terms of talking points and so on."

That would get him out of her hair for a while.

"Do you want me to start talking to the crew?" he asked.

"No. Let's get more information from the head office first," she said. "Then we can take action."

His eyes gleamed with the fervor of a true believer. "Destiny Park will be union-free in no time," he said.

He marched out.

Vanessa peeked out the door to make sure Dirk was gone, then stepped into the office common area. A sudden feeling of being trapped within four walls made her shudder. "How do you get used to working in an office with no windows?" she asked Charlotte, who was busily sorting through a large pile of shift-change requests.

"I go upstairs every once in a while, before I go crazy," Charlotte said.

"Good plan," said Vanessa. She walked over to a rack of handheld radios and picked one up. "Is this how I keep in touch?" She waggled a radio in Charlotte's direction.

"One for you, one for Dirk, one for me, plus a spare. All the attractions have them, too."

Vanessa peered at the dials on the radio. "Got it. Anything else I should know?"

"The area manager's call sign is Legacy. That makes Dirk's call sign Legacy 2. The office's call sign is—"

"Legacy office?" Vanessa guessed.

"Bingo," said Charlotte. "The attraction call signs are just their names: American Dream, Ghost Factory, and Gold Rush."

"Easy peasy," said Vanessa. She patted her clothes, looking for a place to clip the heavy radio. The waistband of her skirt was not ideal, but it would have to do. She made a mental note to start wearing pants instead of skirts. As she smoothed her jacket back into place, she noticed the radio created a large bulge under the fabric. *It looks like I'm packing heat.* She shrugged off the jacket. *Better.*

Free of the office, Vanessa bounded up the stairs and out into Destiny Park. Once outside, she unclipped the radio and pressed the talk button. "Legacy to Legacy office. Do you copy? Over."

Static crackled, then Charlotte's voice came over the radio. "Copy that, Legacy. Over."

"10-4, Legacy office. Thank you. Over." Satisfied with her new toy, Vanessa clipped it back on her skirt waistband and straightened up. *Where to go first?* American Dream was the closest attraction, making it the obvious choice.

She waved and said "Good morning!" to the crew member at the front entrance.

Nonplussed, he tentatively waved back. A gaggle of visitors diverted his attention, demanding to know if there was a line, how long it was, how long the show lasted, and what time the 3:00 parade would start, so Vanessa bypassed the lot of them and went inside without adding to his troubles.

She made a beeline to the break room. Inside, she encountered one lone crew member, a man in his early fifties, sitting contentedly in a chair.

He appeared to be spooning up yogurt from a disposable container.

"Good morning," Vanessa said.

"Hey," said her break room companion, whose name tag read "Bob."

"What are you up to this morning, Bob?" She sat down in the chair next to him.

Unfazed, Bob held up his yogurt container. "You want some custard? It's really good," he said.

Now it was Vanessa's turn to be nonplussed. *What do you say to an offer like that?*

"No, thanks, I just had breakfast—Bob, is it?"

"Yessiree," he said. He took another bite of yogurt. "You're the new manager."

"I am, indeed. You can call me Vanessa."

"All right," he replied. "Vanessa. What can I do for you?"

"I'm just checking in on everybody today. I haven't gotten much of a chance to, what with all the trainings and so on."

He nodded slowly. "You been to the parade yet?"

"I thought I might today, as a matter of fact. Anything else you would recommend?"

He held his spoon suspended in midair while he considered. "Nope."

The spoon resumed its journey.

"That's fine. Thank you, Bob," she said as she went to the break room door. "You have a nice day, now."

After exiting American Dream, she walked over to the roller coaster. The line at Gold Rush already snaked through the waiting area despite the early hour. Instead of entering the loading area, as she had done before with Thomas, she approached the attraction entrance.

"Good morning," she said to the woman at the entrance, whose eyes widened upon being addressed. Her name tag read "Maribel."

"Good morning," Maribel said.

"How's it going over here?"

"Oh, fine!" She glanced over her shoulder to survey the queue, sending her thick brown braid swinging. "Going to be a busy day for sure. See the line?"

"I sure do," said Vanessa. "Were you at the meeting a few days ago? I don't think we've met. I'm the new area manager." She held out her hand to shake.

Maribel shook it. "I wasn't at the meeting, but I heard about it when I came in. Thomas mentioned it."

"Thomas did? Is he here today?"

"No, he's not here today."

Vanessa must have looked visibly disappointed, for Maribel quickly added to her statement. "I mean, he's not *here* today. At Gold Rush. But he's probably at Ghost Factory."

"Really? That's where I was headed next. Thank you, Maribel. You have a good day." *Thomas at Ghost Factory? I wonder if he's training someone.* Her steps quickened.

Outside Ghost Factory, she stopped at a distance to study the exterior. The spiked fence and red brick drew the eye first, but there were many more details if one looked closely. The red brick framed a large clock with Roman numerals and two pointed hands. There were glass windows divided by frames into multiple rows of squares, each pane too opaque to see the interior. The line of visitors wound through the gate and under the clock, looking for all the world like a motley crew arriving for work, albeit dressed in clothes unbefitting a Victorian factory worker.

She dodged the line and entered through the side door. The transition from the bright morning sun to the dark interior of the building made her momentarily blind. She groped along the passageway until her eyes adjusted. *There's the break room.* She reached for the door handle and was just about to pull open the door when she heard a voice.

She froze.

"You've worked here for ten years, but they're giving the new people better shifts than you?"

*Thomas.*

Someone responded too quietly for her to hear.

Determined not to eavesdrop, she pulled open the door and pushed aside the velvet curtain.

## Thomas

Thomas looked up as the curtain whipped aside and revealed Vanessa.

*Oh.*

Determined not to be caught flat-footed, he turned back to his coworker with the blandest expression he could manage. "Happens all the time. You jumping back in now?" he asked, using crew member lingo for going back to work after your break.

The crew member said she was. With a wary glance at Vanessa, she left the break room.

"Hi," Vanessa said to Thomas.

"Hi, yourself." *Clever, Thomas. Really clever.*

"I'm doing a walk-through this morning. Checking out the lay of the land."

"Really? Did you ride Gold Rush again?"

She laughed. "Not this time."

"Missed opportunity," he chided. "You know you want to go see that ghost horse again."

"I did like the ghost horse," she said. "I'll have to do that again sometime."

"Did you already go to American Dream?"

"Went there first. Bob told me not to miss the parade."

"Tall Bob or Short Bob?" asked Thomas.

"I beg your pardon?"

"There's two Bobs. One of them is called Tall Bob, one of them is called Short Bob. So we know who we're talking about."

She looked utterly confused. "The Bobs don't mind being called 'Tall' and 'Short'?"

"Nah. When you get a nickname here, you know you've made it. For better or for worse," he said.

"I think it must have been Short Bob. He was eating yogurt and asked me if I wanted some."

"That's the one! That's Short Bob, for sure. Yogurt fiend."

"Now I know what to get him for Christmas," she said.

Thomas pictured her in a Santa hat, and had to admit the image was not unappealing. He smiled at the thought—and at her joke.

"How about you? What are you up to today? More training?" she asked.

"Me? No training today. Just a carriage wash later."

"What's a carriage wash?"

"Some of us stay late and wipe down all the Ghost Factory carriages after the park closes."

"That's a lot of carriages to wipe down," she said.

"We try to make it fun. We put some music on the PA system." Thomas did the twist without a hint of embarrassment.

"Sounds like a party. Count me in," she said.

*What?* "You wanna stay late and wash carriages?"

"I sure do." She lifted the curtain out of the way, then looked over her shoulder at him. "The best way to learn how this place works, is to work here."

The curtain fell into place as Vanessa exited the room.

After she left, Thomas sat alone in the Ghost Factory break room. The muted cacophony of the attraction soundtrack vibrated through the walls. To the uninitiated, it might have been distracting, but to Thomas it was as familiar as the white noise from an old washing machine.

He folded his arms on the table and rested his head on them.

Vanessa's attendance at the carriage wash held both promise and danger. Thomas felt the knife-edge of his dilemma, sharp and bittersweet, as he contemplated the night ahead.

In front of her, he must be careful not to speak of the union. There would be no opportunity to reach out to his fellow crew members tonight.

Despite that discouraging thought, pleasure crept over him at the memory of spending time with her. It had been a long time since he had enjoyed someone's company so much.

He stood up. A lazy smile touched his lips.

*Danger and promise.*

# Roller Coaster Romance

## Vanessa

"Legacy 2 to Legacy," the walkie-talkie squawked with Dirk's voice.

"Legacy here," she responded.

"What's your 20, Legacy?"

Vanessa remembered the phrase from where she used to work. "What's your 20?" meant "Where are you?"

"Outside Ghost Factory, Legacy 2," she replied.

"Can you return to base?"

"10-4, be right there."

It had been a busy morning, running from American Dream, to Gold Rush, and then to Ghost Factory. The heat of the sun on her back made her view the trip underground more favorably.

At least she could cool off.

Dirk awaited her in the office with a stack of papers. "Here's 'Union-Free for You and Me,' and here's 'Union-Free Toolbox,'" he said, handing over each bundle. "And here's today's parade group." He passed over a single sheet of paper.

She examined the two packets from the head office. *This should make interesting reading.* "Thank you, Dirk. Can you handle any radio calls that come in? I want to go over these materials."

"Of course," he said.

She turned to Charlotte. "Charlotte, is there anywhere underground I could sit and read for a while? Just for a change of scenery?"

"There's an underground break room down the way. You want me to walk you there?"

"That'd be great."

The tinny "Voice of Destiny" echoed overhead as Charlotte led her along a different route through the corridor than Vanessa had used before. This particular corridor dead-ended in a large room filled with beat-up tables, mismatched chairs, and a few sagging sofas. She thought of the glittering castle overhead. *Very different from upstairs.* Televisions set to the local 24-hour news channel perched on stands on opposite sides of the room.

Vanessa sat down on a sofa not currently occupied by a sleeping crew member and paged through one of the packets.

"Know your TIPS and your FOE! Managers may not Threaten, Interrogate, Promise, or Spy on employees. Managers may share verifiable Facts, Opinions, and Examples."

*Did I 'interrogate' Thomas when I asked him about this?* Horrified at the thought of having said the wrong thing, she quickly scanned the text and read the pertinent part aloud to herself: "Managers may not ask associates about their position on unions."

*Damn. I shouldn't have said that.* She put her head in her hand and kept reading. She stopped only to quiet her rumbling stomach with an oatmeal creme pie from the vending machine, which allowed her to collect her thoughts as she nibbled the tasty junk food.

*There's an awful lot of nudging and winking in this stuff. You can't fire someone for union organizing, but you can fire a union organizer for something else as long as you can back it up with documentation. That must be what Dirk was alluding to with his mobster impression.*

Unlike the oatmeal creme pie, it left a bad taste in her mouth.

She gathered up her things and returned to her office, depositing them in a heap on her desk, before making her way upstairs.

## Roller Coaster Romance

The parade route thronged with visitors, many of whom were already claiming front-row seats by laying down towels or using a stroller to block off their very own makeshift VIP section. Vanessa dodged through the crowd and into the American Dream lobby to find her parade crew waiting in the break room.

They crowded around the bulletin board, reading a flyer pinned to the middle. She recognized Bob, the yogurt fiend—she refused to call him "Short Bob," even in the privacy of her thoughts—though "Bob the Yogurt Fiend" was hardly an improvement. The others she did not know.

"Good afternoon, everyone."

Bob and the rest of the crew turned away from the bulletin board to face her.

"I'm Vanessa, the new area manager, and today I'll be supervising our section of the parade route." She unfolded the list of parade route stations and pinned it to the bulletin board next to the flyer. "You'll find your assignments here."

Before turning back to face the crew, she read the neighboring flyer.

> *We said the Gold Rush costume was dangerous.*
> *Why hasn't management listened?*
> *Vote YES to unionize and make safety a priority!*

As soon as she read it, she realized the crew would be watching for her reaction. She adopted a bland expression before facing them.

They looked at her with unabashed curiosity.

She cleared her throat before speaking. "I'll come around and check in with you once you get set up. Any questions?"

No one spoke, although they did steal a few glances at one another.

*Good thing they already know what they're doing.*

"All right, let's head out. Meet back here after the parade."

After checking for their assigned area, the crew filed out of the break room.

Vanessa followed them out and watched as they took up positions along the route.

One applied masking tape to the concrete to create temporary walkways and barriers while another directed visitors in wheelchairs to a special roped-off viewing area. Bob moseyed along the route chatting with visitors. The last few crew members held a rope across the parade route to block visitors from wandering into the path of the oncoming parade.

The afternoon heat poured from the sky and reflected from the ground. Vanessa realized the costumes must be scorching in the heat. Even without her jacket on, she felt sweat accumulate and drip down her spine. She worked her way down the parade route station by station, helping out with the responsibilities of each position, until she heard the parade fanfare.

The music preceded the parade, blaring over the sound system before the parade itself turned the corner from Discovery into Legacy.

> *Journey to Destiny, live your Fantasy,*
> *Build a Legacy. It's all here for you.*
> *A new Discovery awaits*
> *In a Galaxy of adventure.*
> *Journey to Destiny, where dreams come true.*

Just as the music reached a high note, the parade came into view. Vanessa helped the crew members clear the route of the last remaining visitors, who, for unknown reasons, were attempting to cross in front of the oncoming parade. With all of the visitors safely corralled, Vanessa retreated to watch the parade.

The first float, representing the Galaxy area, glittered with hundreds of tiny paillettes worked into a pattern of stars and swirling rainbow space dust. Atop its platform, dancers clad in Mars red or Neptune blue whirled their crystal-encrusted hula hoops like rings orbiting a planet.

On the Discovery float, four tree trunks held aloft a canopy thick with oversized flowers that opened and closed. The dancers wore fanciful stylized animal suits, including a silver-scaled fish and a brown bear who pursued it around the perimeter of the float.

A massive dragon curled in the middle of the Fantasy float. It appeared to be sleeping until it slowly lifted one heavy eyelid and hissed a thin trail of smoke from its nostrils. Around the dragon, a court of belly dancers dressed as shimmering peacocks fluttered their skirts in time to the music. A fountain at each corner of the float burbled a constant stream of water.

Vanessa instantly recognized the final float.

Decorated with four white columns connected by lengths of red, white, and blue bunting, the Legacy float featured a tableau of living statues posed on a set piece crafted to resemble a craggy mountain overlook. The living statue of a miner held his pickax aloft and unmoving for an impossibly long time. Every so often, the statues eased into different positions before freezing in place again.

Only as the final float passed by were the shadowy silhouettes of ghosts visible on the back of the Legacy float, ending the parade with an unsettling stinger.

Released from the viewing area, the visitors milled in all directions.

Vanessa pulled up tape with the rest of the crew until every piece had been removed, then led the way back to the break room.

Everyone collapsed into chairs to recover from the intense heat.

Vanessa took a closer look at the Gold Rush neckerchief around one young woman's neck. "May I borrow that for a moment?" she asked, indicating the accessory.

The young woman regarded Vanessa with surprise. "Sure," she said, removing her hat and peeling the neckerchief off. "It's kinda sweaty," she said, passing it to Vanessa.

Vanessa pulled the neckerchief over her head.

The crew stared.

She tugged on the neckerchief from several directions, feeling it press against her neck as she did so. "It's that it won't come free when pulled, isn't it?" she asked.

Only Bob answered. "Yup. Stupid thing dangles all over the place."

"And what if it got caught in the machinery, right?"

He didn't say anything. He just nodded, which seemed to prompt the owner of the neckerchief to pipe up.

"It should have a Velcro fastener instead of a knot," she said.

Vanessa handed the neckerchief back to her. "I see what you mean." She addressed the group. "Okay, everyone, that's a wrap. Head back to your attraction and I'll see you next time."

The strength of her feelings increased her pace as she strode out of American Dream. *Such a simple, sensible request. Why didn't management address this before?*

She vowed to ask Mr. Destiny as soon as possible.

# CHAPTER 6

## Vanessa

Unsure of what the carriage wash would entail, Vanessa retrieved a spare set of casual clothes from her car and used the locker room to change into jeans and a lightweight plaid work shirt. She checked with Charlotte about ordering pizza for the carriage wash crew and was relieved to find out that pizza delivery would make it unscathed through the park security gate, as long as there was someone to meet the driver in the manager parking lot.

She ordered a pile of cheese and pepperoni pizzas, then fed quarters and bills into the underground break room vending machine until it spit out a sufficient number of sodas. She hauled them back to the office and ran upstairs to receive the pizzas, then staggered downstairs under their weight, her arms heating up uncomfortably from the stack of pizza boxes.

With the pizza safely deposited on the office counter, she unclipped her radio and called Ghost Factory. "Legacy to Ghost Factory."

"Ghost Factory here."

It sounded like Thomas.

"Ghost Factory, can you send someone down to the office to help transport some carriage wash supplies?"

"10-4, Legacy. On my way."

She straightened and re-straightened the stack of pizza boxes. She wiped and re-wiped the condensation that dripped from the sodas. She leaned against the counter, trying to feel calm, until the door finally opened.

"Hey!" said Thomas. "What's all this?"

"Hey, yourself," she said. "I got us some pizza. Thought you all might be hungry."

"Or you and I could just eat it all, right now, and they'd never be the wiser." He rubbed his hands together and laughed like a villain in a movie.

Vanessa rolled her eyes and laughed. "Don't tempt me." She reached for the pizza, but he stepped in front of it.

"What happened to your arm?"

"What?" She looked down. "It's just red from carrying the pizza."

He pulled a handful of paper towels from the nearby dispenser and ran them under the cool water tap in the sink. "May I?" he asked, waiting for her assent before he cradled her forearm in one hand and applied a wet paper towel to the redness with his other hand.

Their eyes met.

"Hold that there," he said.

Vanessa felt the hair stand up on her arm. *Must be the cold towels.* She shivered.

He let go. "Does it hurt?"

"I'm fine, really," she said.

He gave her a skeptical look. "Don't sacrifice a limb just to get us some pizza." He rummaged in a cabinet under the counter and found an old grocery bag, then loaded the sodas into it.

"Let me get that," she said, reaching for the bag.

"Not with your scorched arm," he said.

"Only the good one, I promise."

He relented and handed the bag to her.

"I have an idea. Take off your jacket," she said.

He raised his eyebrows and complied.

She took the Ghost Factory jacket and laid it out on the counter. "Now stack the pizzas on it. That way, your arms will be safe."

They carried the pizza and sodas up to Ghost Factory and laid them out in the break room.

## Thomas

*Still there.* The flyer he'd pinned to the bulletin board in the Ghost Factory break room remained, just visible behind the stack of pizzas. He didn't need to read it to know what it said.

He'd written it.

*We arrive early to put on a costume and stay late to take it off again.*

*Why aren't we paid for this extra time spent working?*

*Vote YES to unionize and stand up for fair wages!*

Short Bob had written the other one. He took the Gold Rush neckerchief personally—not surprising, considering he'd nearly been caught on a ride vehicle just as it was about to launch.

The velvet curtain swung aside and three more crew members crowded into the room.

"Oh, look, the Blondes are here," he said. "Where's your charge, ladies?"

Paulina, Laura, and Claudia giggled in unison. "We left him to find his way," said Paulina.

"Or not!" said Laura.

"Vanessa, this is Paulina, Laura, and Claudia," said Thomas. "Don't get too attached to their names," he said. "They trade name tags constantly."

"Did I hear you call them 'The Blondes'?" Vanessa asked, in a tone that teetered between disapproval and amusement.

Claudia rescued him. "It's our nickname for ourselves." She linked arms with her yellow-haired compatriots. "Right, girls?"

"Right!" they chorused, then doubled over in laughter.

*Ah, the energy of youth.* Thomas snuck a glance at Vanessa, who was smiling, before addressing Claudia again. "Where's Marco? Did you leave him to wander the underground forever?"

"Who's Marco?" Vanessa asked.

"He finished training last week," Thomas replied. "These three talked him into the carriage wash today."

"We took him on a tour," said Paulina.

"A long tour," added Laura.

"Should we go look for him?" asked Vanessa.

The door opened and a young man strolled into the room. The Blondes shouted "Marco!" and surrounded him, hustling him out the break room door and down the hallway. Their boisterous noise echoed back to the break room until the door swung completely shut.

Vanessa looked at Thomas. "Wow," she said.

"Wow is the word," he agreed.

"Where are they taking him?"

"Best not to ask."

She flipped open a pizza box. "More for us, then," she said, and helped herself to a slice of cheese pizza.

"I couldn't agree more." He snagged a handful of paper towels from the dispenser and handed a few to her. "Would you like a plate?"

"You are the wizard of paper towels today, aren't you?" She put her slice on the towel and sat down at the table.

Thomas sat down across from her. *I hope Marco and the Blondes decide to go on another tour. A very long tour.* He racked his brain for something intelligent to say. "Where did we leave off last time?"

"Last time?"

"As I recall, you claimed mythological origins."

Vanessa chuckled. "Right." She put down her pizza. "You already heard about the little family-owned amusement I used to work for. Nothing like this," she gestured to their surroundings. "We had a coaster, a flume, a couple of carnival rides, that sort of thing. Anyway, after a while, the maintenance of keeping the place up cost more than it was bringing in. They had to close it down."

"Then you ended up here."

"Then I ended up here," she said.

"Why move so far? You got family down here?"

She shook her head. "All in Tennessee. Most of 'em in the same county, for that matter."

"You miss it?"

"I miss some things."

"Like what?" *She's left behind a handsome mountain man who splits logs single-handedly. That would be my luck.*

"The mountains. My mom and dad."

*Yes! No mountain man.* "That's not a long list," he said.

"I suppose not." She sighed. "You're from a small town, though—you know what it's like."

"Provincial? Suffocating?"

"Unchanging," she said. "Which isn't a bad thing, necessarily, but..." She trailed off, then looked him in the eye. "Sometimes you want to know what's around the river bend. You know what I mean?"

"Yes," said Thomas. "I know just what you mean."

The four other crew members crashed through the door again and snatched up the unopened pizza boxes.

Marco discovered the bag of sodas and handed them out to all present, including Thomas and Vanessa, who had gone quiet, and the Blondes, who were singing a mildly inappropriate sea shanty.

Thomas, who had looked away from Vanessa during the commotion, looked back at Vanessa.

She held the soda can in her hand, unopened.

He wanted to say something profound, but he settled on something mundane. "I'll get the cleaning supplies," he said. "You go ahead and finish your pizza."

Vanessa started as if she had been woken from a dream. She smiled slowly. "I'll be here," she said, raising her eyebrows to indicate the company into which she'd fallen.

He went out to the hallway and retrieved a small boombox and a caddy of rags and cleaning spray from the supply closet. He carried them to the attraction loading area and set them on top of the ride control cabinet. He plugged in the boombox and fiddled with the dial to tune in the pop station, then cranked up the volume to a sufficient level.

Pleased with his handiwork, he returned to the break room to collect his fellow crew members and Vanessa.

They descended on the loading area in a festive mood. Each person grabbed a rag and went to work wiping down the carriages. When they finished all the carriages in the loading area, Thomas engaged the ride controls to move the ride vehicles forward so that a new set of carriages took their place in the loading area.

Paulina, Laura, and Claudia kept up a happy stream of chatter, carrying Marco along in their wake. Vanessa seemed to half-listen to the conversation as it ebbed and flowed, but she never stopped moving long enough to join in. Thomas fell into sync with her, scrubbing quickly but thoroughly without saying much.

After a while, they stopped for a break. Marco whirled the radio dial in search of a new station. The speakers spit out bits of talk radio and commercials before he landed on a country station.

"Anything but country," Thomas said. "Those are the rules."

"Whose rules? Marco, step aside," Vanessa said. She turned up the volume and bobbed her head to the rhythm.

Laura and Claudia linked arms and skipped in a circle. Paulina grabbed Marco's arm and joined in.

"No, no, that's not how it's done," Vanessa said. "Watch."

She moved to an open part of the loading area and began stepping neatly in time with the song, narrating each step: "Rock step, cha-cha-cha, rock step, cha-cha-cha. Half turn, cha-cha-cha, half turn, cha-cha-cha."

"Wait!" said Thomas.

Vanessa stopped moving.

He reached in the cabinet and pulled out a Gold Rush hat, then placed it on her head. "Perfect."

She smiled and resumed the dance.

The Blondes and Marco began imitating her steps, occasionally turning in the wrong direction, until they got the hang of the movements.

"You can do it with a partner, too," she said as another song began. She gestured for Paulina to stand next to her, then danced the steps in tandem with Paulina. Vanessa pivoted and faced Paulina, never missing a step, then pivoted again and danced in parallel with her.

When Paulina retreated, Marco stepped up and put his hands in the proper position to meet Vanessa's grasp.

Thomas, torn between wanting to take Marco's place and wanting to run away before he made a fool of himself, hung back and watched the others.

"What do you think, Thomas?" called Vanessa as she and Marco rock-stepped and cha-cha'd around the loading area.

"I think you've been holding out on us."

She laughed and spun away from Marco to face Thomas. Her cheeks were pink. She whipped off the hat and offered it to him.

*I can't believe I'm doing this.* He put on the hat.

*Here goes nothing.*

This time, Marco, Paulina, Laura, and Claudia stepped back to give them room.

Thomas watched Vanessa closely, picking up on her cues as she guided their linked hands through the air, catching the intention of her next movement from the tilt of her head or the lean of her body.

When the song finished, they swayed to a stop facing each other. He didn't want to look into her eyes, because he knew what she would see in his, but it was too late.

## Vanessa

She completed the last turn and stopped, facing Thomas. Her breath came too fast. She knew she should let go of his hands, but the look on his face blotted out all rational thought. Before she could stop herself, she squeezed his hands.

His eyes flared with what looked like pure hope.

Realization crashed down on her.

*Oh, no.*

She let go and stepped back. "We'd better get these carriages moving," she said. Her heart raced and her hands trembled as she grabbed the nearest spray bottle and rag.

Thomas crammed the hat back into the cabinet and busied himself setting the carriages in motion. When they stopped, he turned the radio back to the pop station and scrubbed the first carriage like his life depended on it.

She chose the carriage at the opposite end of the loading area, letting Paulina, Laura, Claudia, and Marco take the ones in the middle. The line of carriages stretched on and on—no matter how many she scrubbed, it seemed like there were always more to come.

*How do you know when you're done?* She hadn't thought to note where they started. Surely Thomas had, but she couldn't bring herself to ask him, not with her feelings still roiling from their impromptu duet.

At long last, after every carriage had cycled through the loading area, Thomas shut down the ride for the night.

Marco and the Blondes disappeared out the side door, leaving Thomas and Vanessa alone inside the attraction.

Vanessa gathered up fallen rags while he unplugged the boombox and loaded the supplies back into the caddy. Neither of them spoke. She picked up the boombox and followed him back to the supply closet.

When everything had been stowed inside the closet, Thomas closed the door and leaned against it, facing her.

"I'm sorry," she blurted. "I don't know what came over me. I shouldn't have done that."

He regarded her from across the narrow hallway. "Done what?" A smile pulled at the corners of his lips.

She saw it and lost her concentration entirely. "I … "

Now he was really smiling. "I taught you how to run a roller coaster. You taught me a line dance. It's been a good week, I'd say."

"A good week?" Vanessa echoed. She didn't know what to say to that. *Here I am, trying to apologize for grabbing his hands like a schoolgirl, and he's grinning like a fool.* "A good week," she conceded.

They walked out of the attraction together, the lights in the trees twinkling sedately under a full moon.

He turned to her. "Good night, Vanessa." His gentle tone acknowledged something new between them.

"Good night, Thomas."

They went their separate ways into the deserted park.

## CHAPTER 7

## Vanessa

Vanessa leaned against the weathered wood fence at the Gold Rush overlook, watching the coaster dip and turn. Once you were strapped in, there was no way to turn back. You rode out the peaks and valleys until it was done with you, whether you liked it or not.

She already felt like she'd been on the ride one too many times.

*Once more unto the breach.* Stress brought out the Shakespeare quotes she thought she'd long forgotten.

Vanessa turned from the view and hailed the crew member at the attraction entrance. He was a tall man, and his name tag read "Bob."

She barely managed to stop herself from calling him "Tall Bob."

"Good morning, Bob. I don't think we've met. I'm Vanessa, the new area manager. Can you point me in the direction of the Gold Rush break room?"

"Sure can. Go into the loading area and head to the left, behind the control tower. It's back in there."

"Thank you. You have a good day," she said.

She found it just where he described.

Another union flyer hung on the bulletin board.

> *Have you been punished unfairly by management?*
> *Wish you had someone in your corner to fight for YOU?*
> *We are stronger together! Vote YES to unionize!*

Maribel, the Gold Rush crew member she'd met the other day, sat at a little table with a cup of coffee and a book.

"Hey, Maribel. How's it going?"

Maribel looked up. "Good, you?"

"Fine, thanks. I know you're on a break right now, and I hate to interrupt, but I need a little help."

Maribel put down the book and gave Vanessa her full attention.

"If I can borrow you for five minutes, can you add that five minutes onto your break when we're done?"

"Sure," said Maribel.

"Great. I need you to show me around the loading area a little bit. Point out where the neckerchief is in danger of getting caught."

"Really? We tried to tell them about that before…"

"But they didn't listen," Vanessa said. "I know. I think it's worth another try."

"Is this about the union thing?"

"Maribel, I'm officially not allowed to have an opinion on that. Let's just say that I want to keep you all safe, no matter what."

Maribel raised one eyebrow. "Whatever you say, boss," she said.

They went to the loading area and Maribel showed Vanessa exactly how the accessory could snag on the lap bar or the ride vehicle decorations.

It was such an obvious hazard Vanessa couldn't believe no one had taken the crew's complaint seriously.

"Thank you for showing me," Vanessa said. "Don't forget to take your extra five minutes before you jump back in, okay?"

She left Maribel and went to the Legacy office. "Charlotte, since we get memos from Mr. Destiny, I assume there's a way to send one to him?"

"You can try," Charlotte said. "But he doesn't show up here unless he has to."

"What else does he have to do?" Vanessa asked. She remembered her old amusement park, where the owners practically lived on-site.

Charlotte shrugged. "Jet around and drink champagne, I guess. Beats working in a cave."

"Can you call up to the head office?"

"Sure, I can call anyone you like." Charlotte picked up the handset and dialed an extension. "Hello? Is Mr. Destiny available? The Legacy manager would like to speak with him." She listened. "Thank you. I'll tell her." She hung up. "His secretary said he'll be in and out today, getting ready for an all-hands meeting."

"Another one already?" Vanessa said. "Is that normal?"

"Not in my experience. And"—she leaned across the desk and lowered her voice—"you might want to keep an eye on our friend Dirk. He's been running a lot of 'errands' up there."

"Good to know. I think I'll pay Mr. Destiny a visit myself, before he jets off again."

She detoured to the costume department to pick up a neckerchief before returning upstairs to the Mirror Castle. The hidden elevator carried her to the heart of the head office, but this time, there were no voices to follow. She looked up and down the hallway before heading in the opposite direction of the meeting room. The hallway dead-ended at a desk, staffed by an unsmiling woman wearing a headset.

"My secretary called up earlier. I'm Vanessa, the Legacy manager. May I speak to Mr. Destiny?"

The woman eyed her. "Just a moment." She touched a button on her desk. "Mr. Destiny? The Legacy manager is here to see you." Her hand went to the headset as she listened. "Yes, sir. I'll send her in." She addressed Vanessa. "He'll see you now."

# Thomas

Thomas checked the clock on the wall in the underground break room. *Early. I'm just early. They'll show up.* He drummed his fingers on the arm of the sofa as the television droned on about the weather.

Maribel sat down next to him. "Hey. How's the weather?"

"Cloudy with a chance of getting fired."

"Aren't you the funny one. Where's Short Bob?"

"On his way," Thomas said. "I hope."

"I saw Paulina in costuming. She should be here in a minute. Guess who I saw this morning?"

"Surprise me," said Thomas.

"Vanessa."

Thomas sat up straight. "Where? What did she want?"

"She wanted me to demonstrate that costuming safety issue on Gold Rush," Maribel said.

"Really?" Thomas drew the word out, long and speculative.

"I like her," said Maribel.

Thomas struggled to reduce his opinion to an acceptable response, like *I do, too*, or *She seems nice*, but ran out of time as Paulina and Bob arrived.

Paulina sat down next to Maribel while Bob sank into the armchair adjacent to the sofa.

"Where are we at, people?" asked Paulina.

"We were just discussing Vanessa," said Maribel.

"She's quite the dancer," said Paulina. "Right, Thomas?"

"Thomas? Is there something you want to share with the class?" Maribel elbowed him.

"She showed us a line dance at the carriage wash," he said.

Paulina giggled and made tiny kissing sounds.

"Shut up, Paulina," said Thomas.

"I miss all the fun stuff," said Bob.

"Well, she must have liked your poster, or she wouldn't have come down to Gold Rush," Maribel said.

"True," said Bob.

"Anyway," said Thomas, attempting to keep the conversation on track, "how's it going at your attraction? Maribel?"

Maribel took a folded piece of paper out of her pocket and studied it. "It's pretty good. I'd say we have about fifty percent in favor right now."

"Bob? How's American Dream?"

"We don't have as many crew members as you all do"—he indicated Maribel—"but I think we have about the same split 'for' and 'against.'"

"That leaves Ghost Factory. Paulina, how's it going with your crowd?" Paulina, as Thomas well knew, had a lighthearted exterior along with a canny knack for observing people.

Right now, she was all business. "It's a tie between the people who couldn't care less, and the people who really want a union. Not too many fence-sitters."

"It's close everywhere," he agreed. "Anybody free to do some home visits this weekend?"

"I can," said Maribel.

"Good," said Thomas. "I'll see about getting some more names and addresses. Any ideas for what we can do here at the park? I like the posters, but maybe we can do something new. Keep it fresh."

The organizing committee sat in silence.

The news station broadcast the weather all over again. This time, the forecaster mentioned the formation of a tropical wave.

"That's what we need," said Bob. "A big wave of an idea."

"I think it's time to go public," said Thomas. "Why don't we do our next poster with testimonials? 'Why I'm Voting Yes'?"

"Doesn't that put us at risk?" said Maribel.

"They're going to find out sooner or later who's on the committee," said Thomas. "I wouldn't be surprised if we're already on some list upstairs, but it's against the law to fire us just for trying to organize."

"Maybe so," said Maribel, "but who's to say they can't invent some reason to fire us?"

"It's a risk," Thomas acknowledged. "At least by going public, we give ourselves some protection. It looks fishy if they start firing everyone who's pro-union." He looked at each of them. "Are we all agreed? Next flyer with names and testimonials?"

Maribel, Bob, and Paulina nodded.

"The more support we show, the more we'll get."

# Vanessa

She pushed open the heavy door. Mr. Destiny's leather chair faced away from the massive desk, toward a wall made entirely of glass. The park lay before them like an architectural model, tiny trees and little buildings to scale.

He turned in his chair and stood up, reaching out to shake her hand. "Vanessa. So glad to meet you. Have a seat, won't you? How are you finding Legacy?"

She sat down and placed the neckerchief on her lap, temporarily out of sight. "I love it. I'm thrilled to be here. It's a beautiful park."

"Yes, I'm very proud of it. So what brings you up here today? Didn't I see you at the meeting earlier this week?"

"Yes, sir. I was there. In fact, that's one of the reasons I'm here." She placed the neckerchief on the edge of his desk, careful not to disturb the knick-knacks along the edge. "There have been some flyers in the crew break rooms about the"—she paused to recall his word for it—"situation."

He picked up the neckerchief and began wrapping and unwrapping it around his hand.

She continued. "One of them was about this costume piece. About how it's a safety hazard. The way they put it... well, it seemed like it wasn't a new issue."

"Oh, yeah, I remember that," he said, seemingly unconcerned. "What's the problem?"

She knew she had to tread carefully. "I was thinking that it might be a simple fix to make it safer. With Velcro or something."

He snorted. "Vanessa, how long have you been here?"

"About a week, sir. But I've been in attractions management for over a decade." Despite the implied threat, she couldn't help asserting herself just a little.

"Well, then, you know what it's like," he said. "You give in to their every little whim, before you know it, boom!" He flung the neckerchief down. "They think they own the place. Besides, you know what the optics would be if we gave in on something like this while they're trying to organize?"

She opened her mouth to answer, but he answered his own question.

"Give in on this and they'll think it's because of their little organizing drive. It's a win for them. Makes us look weak."

She silently scooped up the abandoned accessory.

Warming to the subject, he went on. "The key here, Vanessa, is that we are going to be smarter than them. We are going to be stronger than them. And we are going to win this fight no matter what it takes. Do you understand?"

"Yes, sir. I do." *I understand you're an arrogant ass who deserves a swift kick in the pants.*

"I know this is a lot to walk in on. But don't worry, we're going to get you up to speed." He smiled benevolently and stood up to walk her to the door. "Our next meeting will feature a very special guest who's going to put an end to this situation once and for all."

After exiting Mr. Destiny's office, Vanessa remained composed all the way to the elevator. As it descended, she leaned her head against the wall, resisting a sudden temptation to bang her forehead against it in frustration.

By the time the door opened, she straightened up to appear unfazed. It was only a short walk to the underground break room, where she could attempt to drown her sorrows with a soda. She rounded the last corner before the break room with impatient speed and ran right into Thomas.

*Not now. Not now!* Her thoughts fell to pieces. It didn't help that he smelled like Christmas.

She twisted the neckerchief in her hands.

The motion caught his eye.

"You wearing a costume today?" he asked.

"This?" She held it up and looked at it like she'd never seen it before. "Oh, no. I just—I was just taking this back to the costume department."

He seemed to be struggling to find something to say. "Right. Yes," he said.

"I'm sorry I ran into you like that. I was in such a hurry," she said.

"No! It's fine. Really. It's fine." He didn't say anything else, but he didn't walk away, either.

*Say something intelligent, Vanessa.* "Well, I must be going," she said with far more cheer than she felt.

"Of course," he said. He turned and extended his arm, like an usher, so she could walk past him.

*Could that have gone any worse?* Inside the break room, she pushed coins into the vending machine. By the time the soda fell out, she realized she didn't even want it anymore.

*Maybe Charlotte would like it.* Vanessa walked back to the Legacy office and found Charlotte facing the copier, cramming a stack of photocopies into her purse. "Charlotte?"

Charlotte whirled around and hid her purse behind her back.

Vanessa held out the can of soda. "You thirsty? I bought it for myself, but I changed my mind."

Charlotte came back to her desk and dropped her purse in the drawer. "I would love a soda. Thank you, Vanessa." She took the proffered can and popped the tab. "How'd it go with the man upstairs?"

"About as well as you'd expect."

"You get shot down?"

"You could say that." Vanessa dropped the neckerchief on Charlotte's desk for emphasis.

Charlotte sipped her soda and looked at Vanessa over her glasses. "Do tell," she said, settling back in her chair.

Vanessa told. It was good to talk to someone.

She left out the part about running into Thomas.

"Sounds like he's bringing some kind of consultant in," said Charlotte.

Vanessa, who was still thinking about her run-in with Thomas, became momentarily confused. "Who?"

"Mr. Destiny."

"Oh. Yes, I think so."

"And there's another meeting." It was a statement, not a question.

"With the consultant," Vanessa said. "Whoever they are."

"What are you going to do?" asked Charlotte.

"I don't know. Keep trying, I guess."

Charlotte picked up the neckerchief. "You know what? Let me run this back down to costuming for you. You take a load off for a few minutes, at least until the next crisis rolls in."

"You don't have to do that," Vanessa said.

"I insist. It's the least I can do," said Charlotte. And with that, she retrieved her purse and went out the door.

## Thomas

From his seat in the theater, Thomas spotted Charlotte coming through the back entrance of American Dream.

He leapt up to meet her. "Did you get it?" he asked in a hushed tone.

"I got it." She pulled the papers out of her purse and handed them over.

"Thank God," he said, flipping through the pages.

She shook her head. "There's a problem, though."

"What do you mean?"

"She saw me," said Charlotte.

"Who saw you?"

"Vanessa. She walked in right as I was putting those in my purse."

*Damn.* "What did she say?"

"Nothing. She just offered me a soda. Then I got her talking about her chat with Mr. Destiny. She tried to talk to him about the costume safety stuff. It didn't go well."

"Surprise, surprise. Still, points for trying. How'd you get free?"

"I offered to take the neckerchief back," she said.

"Nice. Anything else?"

The show was winding up.

"She said the next all-hands meeting has a special guest. Some kind of consultant," said Charlotte.

"A union buster, no doubt. Things are about to get complicated," said Thomas. "Let me know if you hear anything else. And watch out for Dirk. I've seen him skulking around up here. He's up to something."

## Vanessa

Vanessa waited until she was sure Charlotte was gone. She opened the lid of the copy machine. Charlotte had removed her copies, but in her haste, she'd left one of the original papers in the machine.

It contained a list of crew member names and home addresses.

Vanessa studied the list, then carefully placed it back on the glass just as she'd found it.

# CHAPTER 8

## Vanessa

Dirk charged into the office and brandished a flyer at Vanessa. "Have you seen this? 'Why Legacy Crew Members Are Voting Yes.' Guess who's on it?"

Vanessa snatched the paper from his hand.

He crossed his arms and watched her read it.

> *Why Legacy Crew Members Are Voting Yes*
> *My hours got cut again. –Paulina*
> *Health care costs so much I can't afford to go to the doctor. –Bob*
> *Management doesn't respect me when I go to them with an issue. –Maribel*
> *Our wages aren't high enough to cover basic living expenses. –Thomas*
> *Vote YES and stand together for better working conditions!*

"I found that one in the Ghost Factory break room," he said.

"There's probably one in Gold Rush and American Dream, too," Vanessa said as she studied the flyer.

"I'll go take them down," Dirk said.

"No. Leave them alone. We have other priorities."

Vanessa thought fast. *These must be the Legacy organizers. Thomas. Maribel from Gold Rush. Bob from American Dream. And Paulina from Ghost Factory.* "Mr. Destiny wants to use American Dream for the all-hands meeting this afternoon."

"Why not the usual meeting room?"

"He wants everyone there. Area managers, assistant managers, management interns, you name it. All supervisors."

"Must be big," Dirk said.

"See what you can do about making sure everything is clean and in good working order for the meeting. I don't want any surprises," said Vanessa.

"On it," said Dirk. He left.

Vanessa went into her office and closed the door. She sat down and laid the flyer on her desk.

*Thomas.* She remembered his offhand remark about a living wage, and how he refused to admit to an opinion on the union when—unknowingly—she asked him that forbidden question.

The evidence of his allegiance tangled with the memory of his hands in hers on the night of the carriage wash.

It was all too much.

She cradled her head in her hands. *What am I going to do?*

She had no good answer.

Being a manager put her squarely on Mr. Destiny's side whether she wanted to be or not. She feared what he would ask her to do.

*There must be a way to protect my crew and keep my job.* To do that, however, she needed more than information.

She needed help.

Charlotte wasn't on the flyer, but she had to be involved. Her furtive photocopying couldn't be a coincidence. She had no personal need for employee names and addresses.

The only possible explanation was that someone needed them for the organizing effort.

"Charlotte?" she called.

Charlotte opened the door. "Yes?"

"Have you seen any of these around?" She held up the flyer and watched Charlotte's expression.

Charlotte might have made a good poker player. "Nope. Why?"

"Just curious. Dirk took this one out of the Ghost Factory break room."

"Is he supposed to do that?" asked Charlotte.

"As a matter of fact, no. He's not. That's why I was wondering if any other union flyers had gone AWOL."

Charlotte's expression turned even more unreadable, as if she was reacting on the inside but was determined not to let it show. "Is that all? I was about to take my break." She gestured to the spiral notebook she held.

"Of course, go ahead."

Charlotte turned away, then stopped in mid-step and turned back to Vanessa. "You want to come upstairs for a minute?"

"I don't want to horn in on your break," said Vanessa, unwilling to impose even though fresh air and friendly company sounded like the most wonderful thing in the world.

"Nonsense," Charlotte said. "I have something I want to show you. Put your name tag away; we're going incognito."

They both removed their name tags and made their way upstairs to an area of Discovery that Vanessa had not explored, where a thicket of bamboo surrounded a diminutive stone building.

The sign above the entrance read "Coffee Garden." Through the open doorway, they entered a room filled with strange devices made of glass and metal.

"They're all coffee machines," Charlotte said. "I come up here to get the good stuff. You have to take your name tag off, though, since we're not allowed to eat or drink in view of the visitors."

Vanessa studied the menu board. *Americano? French press? Flat white?* Accustomed to whatever came out of the industrial-size coffee machine in the break room, she was at a loss to choose.

Charlotte must have noticed her hesitation. "Have you ever had a Vietnamese iced coffee?" she asked.

"No, I don't think so," said Vanessa.

"You'll love it. Two Vietnamese iced coffees, please," she said.

"Let me," Vanessa said, reaching into her pocket for cash.

"You don't have to—" Charlotte started, but Vanessa had already paid for the coffees.

"I insist. You've been so helpful. It's the least I can do," said Vanessa.

They carried their coffees through the rear of the store and into an enclosed garden, open to the sky but surrounded by bamboo. The bamboo canes knocked against each other, creating the effect of a chorus of wooden wind chimes around the cafe tables and chairs.

Vanessa dipped a long spoon into the tall glass of coffee. It landed in a thick, cream-colored syrup at the bottom. She withdrew the spoon and tasted it. "It's sweetened condensed milk!"

she said. She stirred the spoon into the condensed milk, sending it swirling through the dark coffee.

Charlotte opened the notebook she'd brought with her. "See this? I made this last time I was here." She slid the notebook across the table.

The notebook lay open to a pencil sketch of the seating area, complete with bamboo and hanging lights, with the shop in the background.

Vanessa marveled at the intricate details. "Charlotte, this is wonderful. I had no idea you were an artist. May I look at the other drawings?"

"Be my guest." Charlotte sat back and sipped her coffee.

Vanessa paged through the rest of the notebook, passing sketches of the Mirror Castle and Ghost Factory, along with other locations she didn't recognize.

"You should do something with this," said Vanessa. "You have a real gift."

"Thank you," said Charlotte. "I wanted to join the art department here, but it's hard to get in without a degree. Or some kind of connection in the department."

"Are you going to school for art?"

"A little bit at a time. It's not easy to go to school full-time when you're already working a full-time job," Charlotte said.

"I hear that." She felt the effect of the caffeine take hold. It made her want to jump up and fix something. Anything. To solve all the problems in the world.

*Too bad it's only coffee, not magic.*

## Thomas

Thomas had just finished the pre-show spiel when Dirk strode into the American Dream lobby.

"Thomas," said Dirk, by way of greeting.

"Dirk." Thomas acknowledged him with barely concealed loathing. "What can I do for you?" *Other than help you take a long walk off a short pier, that is.*

"We need to make sure the theater is ready for a very important meeting this afternoon," said Dirk.

"Is that the royal 'we,' Dirk, or are you referring to someone other than yourself?" Thomas tread the border between humor and sarcasm.

"Very funny. Vanessa wants it cleaned up and shipshape. So get some trash grabbers and some brooms and dustpans and get any detritus off the floor. And pass the word to the rest of today's crew, got it?"

"Pick up trash. Got it."

Dirk squinted at him as if trying to determine if he was being mocked in some way.

Thomas grabbed the nearest dustpan and broom and swept up invisible bits from the carpet, all the while whistling the American Dream theme song. He continued the charade until Dirk turned on his heel and marched out. Then, he ditched the broom and dustpan, opened the theater door, and loped down to where Bob sat.

"Bob, it's on. The meeting is today," he whispered, trying to keep his voice down while also being heard over the noise of the show.

"So? What are we gonna do about it?" Bob asked.

"I want to hear what they say."

"You can't do that. They'll see you," said Bob.

"I'll be careful," said Thomas.

Bob shook his head. "You'll get yourself fired, is what you'll do."

After the exchange, Thomas counted the minutes until his shift ended. At closing time, he sped down to the locker room to change. Attired in casual clothing, he made his way upstairs and through the park, blending with the remaining visitors who hadn't found their way to the park exit.

At American Dream, he went in the back way, climbed up on the show stage, and pushed the heavy velvet curtain aside. Looking around one last time to make sure he was unobserved, he stepped through the opening, closing the gap behind him. He picked his way across the platforms that made up the stage until he reached the back wall.

Surrounded by eerily still mechanical figures and hidden by the thick velvet curtain, all he had left to do was wait.

## Vanessa

The last lingering edge of caffeine kept Vanessa on her toes as the managers of Destiny Park gathered in the American Dream lobby.

Vanessa worked her way through the room, making up for lost time at the last meeting, in which the crowded meeting room had put a damper on greetings and conversation. Unlike the Mirror Castle, this was her turf. She could schmooze with the best of them.

One of the doors to the theater opened. Mr. Destiny stuck his head out and called to Vanessa.

She hurried over. "Yes, sir?"

"Vanessa, we're having trouble bringing the lights up in the front of the house. Can you see if you can find the right switch?"

"Absolutely."

"Thank you." He clapped her on the shoulder, then retreated into the theater.

She had no idea where to find that particular switch—or any switch other than the ones Thomas had already shown her. Due to the nature of the meeting, there were no crew members in the building to enlighten her. She followed Mr. Destiny into the theater.

"I'll be right back," she said, attempting to appear confident. She double-checked the control box to see if there were any extra light controls she hadn't noticed before.

There weren't.

She traced the edge of the stage and examined the sides of the proscenium arch. *No luck. Where else could they be?*

The velvet curtain loomed before her. She climbed onto the edge of the stage and pushed past it.

The floor beneath her was not like a normal stage. Instead, it was a series of platforms containing the mechanical elements of the show, with dangerous gaps in between. She concentrated on placing her feet squarely on one platform after another.

A movement in the shadows startled her.

*What was that?*

She turned, but carefully, making sure she didn't slip.

It was Thomas.

With one finger to his lips, and one hand reaching out to implore silence, he straightened to his full height on a platform just a few steps away.

"What are you doing here?" she hissed.

He stepped quietly across the platforms and onto hers.

It seemed very small for two people to share.

"You were waiting for the meeting, weren't you?" she said, taking care to keep her voice low.

"I had to know what they were going to do," he whispered.

"'They'? You know I'm one of 'them,' right? What am I supposed to do with you? They're waiting for me to fix the lights right now." Even in a whisper, she managed to spit the last two words with force.

"I'm sorry," he said. "I didn't mean to get you involved."

"I should fire you right now."

"Please don't. Not when we're having this much fun," he said.

The absurdity of the situation tipped her panic into an unstoppable rush of hysterics. She pressed her lips together to stifle the laughter that bubbled up from deep inside.

Thomas looked at her as if she'd lost her mind, which only made it worse.

When he caught on, and his shoulders began shaking with silent laughter, Vanessa lost it completely.

They clutched at each other as much for balance as to bury the sound of their mirth, her head on his shoulder, and his on hers.

When they regained control, they looked at each other with eyes streaming with tears of laughter. "Just tell me where the front of house light switch is, will you?" whispered Vanessa.

"There isn't one," he whispered in her ear.

"What? Are you kidding? All this for nothing?"

"I wouldn't call it nothing," he said. He winked at her and stepped back into the shadows.

Vanessa carefully picked her way to the front of the stage, pushed aside the curtain, and closed it hurriedly behind her. She climbed down from the edge of the stage and landed safely on solid ground.

Only then did she notice that while she'd been behind the curtain, the theater had filled up.

Mr. Destiny waited just a few feet away, talking to a well-dressed woman Vanessa didn't recognize.

"Mr. Destiny," Vanessa said, a little out of breath. "There isn't a separate switch for the lights. They're either all on, or all off."

"Fine," he said, checking his watch. "Let's get started."

Vanessa took a seat.

Mr. Destiny stepped forward. "Thank you for coming, everyone. You all know the situation we face here at Destiny Park. I want to introduce someone who will be helping us stay union-free."

The unknown woman walked to his side.

"This is Amy Aldrich from Tradimus Labor Consultants. Amy, take it away." He retreated to the side of the theater.

The consultant stood before the assembled supervisors. The house lights created strange patterns of light, highlighting the sleek chignon of her chestnut hair while casting shadows under her cheekbones. "Thank you." She paused, as if gathering her thoughts, then relieved the tension with one dramatic statement.

"You are at war," she said. "You stand on the front line of a conflict for the very soul of Destiny Park. Nothing—absolutely nothing—is more important than your role in keeping Destiny Park union-free."

She paced across the front of the theater, deliberately making eye contact with manager after manager. "If you fail, you and your crew will suffer forever after, separated from one another, the precious relationship that bound you together torn to shreds."

*Good grief.* It took a physical effort for Vanessa not to roll her eyes.

The consultant continued. "What is a union, anyway?"

Vanessa knew better than to volunteer an answer.

Others did not.

The consultant pointed to one of the raised hands.

The selected manager piped up, "An organization for workers."

"Accurate, but not in the truest sense. A union, ladies and gentlemen, is a business. And what does a business need to do?"

Someone called out "Make money!"

The consultant smiled for the first time. "Now we are at the core of the apple," she said. "A union is a business that needs to make money. And how do they make money? Do they make and sell a product? Do they create an amusement park for the enjoyment of all?" She let the last statement hang in the air.

"No, my friends, they do not. The only way a union can make money is to take it from hard-working employees like yours. And what do your hard-working employees get for their dollar?" She raised empty palms to the crowd. "Nothing but a wall. A wall between them and management. No longer can they work things out with you like the adults that they are. Instead, a union controls how they deal with you. No longer can they be promoted on the basis of merit; instead, lazy employees who have been here longer get promoted ahead of bright and eager employees who turn in the best performance. This is a war against the hard work that you do and the hard work your employees do."

Vanessa snuck a covert look around to see how the other managers were reacting.

Some appeared inspired; others, bored.

"I can see," the consultant said, "that some of you are afraid. Afraid you won't know what to say, or what to do. I'm here to tell you that you don't need to be afraid. You can't deliver threats, but I will teach you how to turn up the pressure without breaking the law. You can't interrogate, but I'll teach you how to get information without asking questions. We will supply everything to say, everything to do, to give you the power to save your crew members from the union."

Vanessa wondered what Thomas thought about that.

"You, ultimately, will be the heroes who keep Destiny Park union-free. I will be on-site to help you, and if you have any questions, or feel unsure about your role, please come see me. I would love to speak with you. And now, I'll turn it back over to Mr. Destiny."

"Thank you, Amy," said Mr. Destiny. "She'll be meeting with all of you, area by area, over the next few days. Together, we will win. Thank you all for coming, and be sure to see Amy after the meeting if you have any questions."

As the host of the meeting, Vanessa had a legitimate reason to linger in the theater until everyone had left. She busied herself with a broom and dustpan for several minutes after the theater had emptied.

The velvet curtain twitched.

"All clear," Vanessa said.

Thomas clambered down from the stage.

"You get all that?" she asked.

"Yeah. Yeah, I did," he said.

"You should go," said Vanessa.

"I know." He didn't move.

"Someone could come back," she said. She sat down heavily in one of the seats.

"They could," he said. He sat down next to her.

They sat side by side, not looking at one another, lost in their own thoughts.

"I should go." Vanessa sighed. "She called it 'war,' you know. I don't know how much else I can do. I'm afraid I've already done too much." She put her hand out to the armrest to stand up, without noticing that his hand was already there. The contact comforted her for a fraction of a second before she pulled away and stood up.

He stood up too. "I know. Thank you."

Without another word, Thomas went out the back way.

Vanessa went out the front.

## CHAPTER 9

*Vanessa*

A new memo awaited her when she arrived at the office the next morning.

> *Vanessa Jones*
> *Legacy Management*
> *Destiny Park*
>
> *Dear Ms. Jones,*
>
> *We would like to provide your crew members with an enhanced Halloween party. Your budgetary allowance has been increased to cover the costs. Contact Events Management to reserve your preferred location and arrange for catering.*
>
> *Regards,*
> *Mr. Destiny*

"Charlotte," said Vanessa, "what do they usually do for a Halloween party here?"

"What Halloween party?" said Charlotte.

"Not a usual thing, then?"

"No."

"Thought so." Vanessa handed Charlotte the memo to read for herself.

"Why do we get a big party now?" asked Charlotte, after reading the memo.

"I can't imagine," said Vanessa, even though she had her suspicions. "Might as well make the best of it. Can you get on the horn to Events Management and see what the options are?"

"Can do," said Charlotte, placing the memo in the inbox on her desk.

The radio on Vanessa's hip squawked, interrupting their conversation. "All units please go to channel 2. Repeat: all units please go to channel 2 for an important announcement."

"That's never happened before," Vanessa said as she fiddled with the channel dial.

"Must be something important," said Charlotte.

Vanessa set the radio on the desk so they could both hear it clearly. "Attention all units. The National Hurricane Center is expected to issue a hurricane watch for the coast of Florida within the next day. All areas should plan to execute hurricane ride-out procedures. Additional weather-related instructions specific to your department will be issued shortly. Please return to channel 1 at this time."

"What's a hurricane ride-out?" asked Vanessa.

"Some of the crew—and a manager; that's you—stay at the park for the hurricane. You tie down stuff that could go flying, then you hunker down in one of the attractions and stay there during the storm. After the storm, you go out and clean up so the park can open as soon as possible."

"Oh," said Vanessa, who had never been in a hurricane, let alone ridden one out inside a theme park.

The thought did not appeal to her.

"Kind of like a slumber party," said Charlotte. "With a hurricane outside."

"Who would volunteer for that?" Vanessa's instincts told her to get on a plane and go home before the hurricane arrived.

"You'd be surprised. Some people think it's fun. A badge of honor, really."

Vanessa felt queasy. "I'm going to go watch the weather. I'll be back in a minute."

The familiar drone of the local news reached her before she even entered the underground break room. Once inside, she detoured to the snack machine for an oatmeal creme pie, righteously forgoing an accompanying soda. She settled into one of the chairs facing the TV.

She waited through the local weather forecast, then through another ten minutes of unrelated news, before they finally started the tropical forecast. Vanessa nibbled her oatmeal creme pie and noted the newscaster used the phrase "hunker down" far too often.

All in all, the forecast was less than informative. According to the news, a hurricane was indeed headed toward Florida. It might be a Category 1, or possibly a category 5, upon landfall. Landfall, for that matter, could take place anywhere between Key West and the Florida–Georgia line.

Vanessa nearly threw the remainder of her oatmeal creme pie at the TV, but thought better of it.

## Thomas

"Scuse us, coming through," said a man in a workman's jumpsuit with "Engineering" stitched above his shirt pocket.

Thomas flattened himself against the wall to let the men pass by with a large dolly bearing a brand new water cooler.

Curious, he followed them down the hallway to the Gold Rush break room where he had left his current trainee.

They maneuvered the water cooler off the dolly, twisted it into position, and plugged it in. "Mind giving a hand, mate?" asked one of the men.

Thomas gamely followed them through the hallway to a cart stacked high with large containers of water.

It took two men to carry one jug. Together with Thomas and the trainee, they carried two jugs to the break room. The workmen peeled the cap off one jug and tipped it into the water cooler, which made a loud glugging noise as the water and air equalized.

Thomas popped a cup from the attached dispenser and triggered the tap.

"It'll cool down in a bit," said one of the workmen.

Thomas sipped from the cup. "Why did we get one?" he asked.

"Mr. Destiny ordered them. Said every break room gets one. Big pain, though, carting them in."

"Why now? We've been asking for water coolers for years," said Thomas.

The workman gave him a look. "Why do you think? You guys are trying to unionize, right?" He waved his hand at the water cooler. "He's trying to play nice so you think you don't need to. That's the game, isn't it?" He chuckled as he wheeled the dolly away. His companion followed him out.

Left alone with his trainee, Thomas crumpled the empty paper cup into a hard ball and hurled it into the trash can.

"I heard about that," the trainee said. "The union thing."

Thomas turned to him. "Yeah? What did you hear?"

"They're giving out free t-shirts underground. They say 'Vote No.' Anybody can have one."

Thomas felt like he'd just gone down a steep drop on the roller coaster. "Listen, why don't you go shadow Maribel at the front entrance for a few minutes. I have to run an errand."

Free of his trainee, he moved as fast as he could without drawing attention to himself, taking the stairs two at a time until he reached the underground corridor. No sooner had he turned down the main hallway than he saw a table piled high with t-shirts in all sizes. Crew members from a variety of departments stood before the table, holding up one shirt after another to find the right size.

*After all, money is tight for most of us, and a free shirt is a free shirt. Damn it.*

What he wouldn't do for an unlimited budget. He'd print a thousand "Vote Yes" t-shirts. He'd take out radio and TV ads by the dozen, print a thousand leaflets and hire an army to leave them on every car in the crew member parking lot. He'd hire a plane and write "Vote Yes" across the sky above Destiny Park.

Instead, he stood helplessly by as one crew member after another collected a free t-shirt and ambled away.

## Vanessa

After far too many hurricane updates, Vanessa stalked out of the break room.

Back in the office, she searched her bookshelves for relevant manuals. "Hurricanes," she said. "Weather? Disasters?" She seized a binder labeled "Disaster Preparedness" and hauled it off the shelf, dropping it on her desk with a thud. "Lovely," she said, paging through the dire material and promising herself to read it later.

In the meantime, Charlotte had delivered a packet from Events Management. The packet contained statistics on one of the event spaces available for the Halloween party: occupancy, square footage, catering and bar equipment. It did not, however, contain any photos. The only descriptive information to be found was the name of the space.

"Aquarium Room," she read aloud.

She recalled that Discovery had an aquarium-themed attraction. Could there be a hidden room inside the aquarium?

She called Events Management and spoke to an event coordinator, who agreed to meet her at the attraction in a few minutes. Vanessa emerged upstairs in Discovery, near the Coffee Garden, and followed the signs through a tunnel filled with green vines and blooming orchids. The tunnel opened to reveal a rock facade glinting with dozens of waterfalls, large and small.

The sign, crafted in blue glass mosaic, read "Aquaverse."

Vanessa faced the entrance and felt the mist from the waterfalls blow into her face. Although refreshing, it brought her no closer to discovering the Aquarium Room, so she approached the crew member stationed at the entrance.

"Where would I find the Aquarium Room?" she asked.

The crew member directed her to a side entrance that led to a hallway skirting the perimeter of the attraction. A flight of stairs took her up one more level to reach a plain set of double doors. She pushed one open and stepped inside.

The dark room smelled of wood and water. Vanessa groped for a light switch. The lights revealed a circular room with a broad middle column, like a wagon wheel with an oversized spoke. The wood-paneled outer walls added a luxurious touch.

The event coordinator bustled into the room before Vanessa had a chance to explore. "This your first company party?" she asked.

"Yes," said Vanessa. "This is quite a space."

"Usually it's reserved for corporate clients. I'm surprised they're letting it go to the crew members," the coordinator said. "Of course, it will look even better when it's dressed."

"Dressed?"

"We bring in plants, lights, table decorations, the works," said the coordinator.

Vanessa was impressed. "But why is it called the Aquarium Room?"

"Didn't you know?" The coordinator reached for an untouched light switch. As she flipped it on, the central column lit up from the inside, revealing a glowing cylindrical aquarium teeming with sea life.

As Vanessa watched, a shark spiraled lazily up the column.

## CHAPTER 10

*Vanessa*

With the hurricane preparations complete, Vanessa never wanted to hear the phrase "hunker down" again for the rest of her life.

She double-checked the list of ride-out volunteers, all of whom she didn't know.

Except one.

The final roster included Vanessa, a handful of college-aged crew members, and Thomas.

*A slumber party with a hurricane outside,* Charlotte had said.

Unbidden, the thought of Thomas in red plaid flannel pajamas sprang to mind.

She imagined her pajamas to be green, and printed with flying coffee cups.

Vanessa rubbed her eyes as if to clear away the thought. After one last, absurd picture of the two of them clinking mugs of hot chocolate brimming with marshmallows, she was able to concentrate on the task at hand.

The hurricane bore down with a trajectory predicted to bring the eye directly over the middle of the state.

From what Vanessa understood from the news, the park would be spared the harshest effects, but would still receive a lashing of rain and high winds—even tornados.

She ran one finger down her supply list. The catering department would lay in a supply of nonperishable goods, in case the power went out. The engineering department had already delivered a box of supplies, including flashlights and zip ties, to augment the cleanup bags dropped off by the gardening crew.

Dirk knocked on the frame of the open door. "How's it going?" he asked.

"Fine, all things considered," she said. She almost asked him why he hadn't signed up for the ride-out, but stopped when she realized the question might encourage him to join them. Instead, she stuck to safer ground. "Is everything a go for the Halloween party?"

"All set. I picked the menu; hope you don't mind."

"That's fine. I've had enough to do, what with the hurricane and all. What's on the menu?"

"The Briny Buffet: a seafood extravaganza," he said.

"Fitting. Can you get some party posters up in the crew break rooms, please?" She would have assigned him to run an errand to Nebraska if she could have gotten away with it.

"Will do. Say, when are we meeting with the consultant?" he asked.

The Nebraska idea looked better every second.

"I think it's on hold till after the hurricane. For obvious reasons," she said.

"Right, right," he said.

"Did you need anything else?"

"No. Wait. Yes. Are we dressing up for the party?"

"As in formal wear?" she said.

"As in Halloween costumes," he clarified.

Speechless, Vanessa stared at Dirk. She realized her mouth had fallen open. "Is that the usual procedure?"

"We don't usually have a Halloween party, so … " He let the sentence trail off.

She realized Dirk was dying to dress up.

Vanessa was dying to know what on earth he planned to wear.

The only way to find out was to say yes.

## Thomas

Thomas retrieved another stroller blocking the path to Ghost Factory and parked it against a nearby wall.

Moving strollers was like a never-ending game of whack-a-mole.

As he contemplated flinging the next offending stroller into the nearest decorative pond, he noticed Dirk approaching from the Legacy plaza.

The spring in his step made Thomas instantly suspicious.

Even worse, Dirk was whistling.

Thomas stomped the stroller brake with a little more force than necessary, and nearly jumped when Paulina tapped him on the shoulder to relieve him. He was supposed to go straight to the next position in the attraction, but with his curiosity piqued, he hurried toward the break room instead.

Perhaps he could find out the reason for Dirk's unusual demeanor.

By the time Thomas got to the break room, Dirk had already left. There was, however, a new flyer on the bulletin board. Thomas cringed, expecting it to be a new anti-union screed.

Instead, the bright orange flyer contained only the details of the upcoming Halloween party. "Halloween costumes optional," he read. "Dinner will be provided. Cash bar."

Mr. Destiny's generosity—or his attempt to win over the crew—apparently did not extend to an open bar.

On the way to his next position, Thomas lamented the lack of interesting Halloween costumes for men.

Still, he was sure he could come up with something suitable for the occasion.

## CHAPTER 11

*Vanessa*

The younger volunteers on the ride-out crew tumbled into the American Dream theater like a litter of puppies.

Vanessa and Thomas trailed them, walking side by side.

Everyone dropped their blankets, pillows, and bags in heaps along the aisles of the theater. They had only an hour or so until sundown, at which time they were supposed to retreat into the theater and take cover for the duration of the hurricane.

Vanessa distributed handfuls of zip ties.

The crew fanned out across Legacy, tying garbage cans to fences and gathering up odds and ends to bring inside the attractions. By the time they were done, they dripped with sweat.

Even still, a party atmosphere prevailed. Vanessa had to stop one of the crew members from playfully tying up another with spare zip ties.

As the sun set, the clouds glowed an unusual yellow color that faded to green in the shadows. The park itself took on an otherworldly appearance as the patterns of sunlight and darkness shifted with each passing band of clouds.

Rather than lock everyone inside American Dream before the storm arrived, Vanessa judged it best to let them burn off some energy running around the park. With their outdoor tasks complete, she released the crew members with strict orders to return before dark.

She caught Thomas smiling at her mother hen act. "Aren't you going to go run around?" she asked.

"With them?" He indicated the crew members who were now skipping down the empty street. "I'd rather take a leisurely stroll. It's not every day you get to see the park in this light."

"True," Vanessa said. "I haven't gotten to walk around much."

"Want to go exploring?"

"Sounds like fun. As long as we get back before the skies open up," she said.

"Deal."

From the Legacy plaza, they walked past Ghost Factory to reach Fantasy. The abandoned stalls of the bazaar lacked their usual cloth hangings, giving the marketplace the appearance of having been hastily abandoned.

They sat together on the edge of the outdoor stage, facing the empty bazaar.

"You should catch the show here sometime," said Thomas.

Vanessa peered around for a clue to the show's content. "Really? What is it?"

"Just a dance show." Thomas shrugged. "But it's pretty good. I go every Friday after work."

"I'll have to do that," she said.

They sat and watched the clouds roll by.

"You like caramel corn?" he asked, apropos of nothing.

"Sure, who doesn't?" she said.

"The bazaar has the best. You gotta try it," he said.

"Now you're making me hungry." Vanessa scooted off the edge of the stage and stood up. "Distract me, before I give up our tour and start breaking into the hurricane rations."

"Your wish is my command." He hopped down.

Exiting Fantasy, they approached the Mirror Castle's east elevation. The roiling sky reflected in the mirrors, making the castle itself appear to be formed of storm clouds and eerie light.

They followed a twisting pathway through a rose garden.

Vanessa stopped to inhale the scent from a cluster of pale pink blossoms. "A rose by any other name would smell as sweet," she quoted.

"That's Juliet's line," he said.

"I know. It's quite a speech. 'Romeo, doff thy name; and for that name, which is no part of thee, take all myself.'"

His gaze met hers.

Thomas broke away only to reach for the roses she had released. He leaned down, closed his eyes, and breathed the fragrance of the petals.

## *Thomas*

The downpours of rain became more frequent, echoing loudly on the roof of the theater.

Thomas unrolled his sleeping bag behind the last row of seats. The other crew members claimed the floor in front of the stage.

Someone had thought to bring board games. Happy shouts drifted from the front of the theater as one or another crew member gained a point.

Restless, Thomas went into the lobby. He found Vanessa at the window, watching the storm.

The wrinkle between her eyebrows deepened as the branches of the trees in the plaza whipped back and forth in the windy darkness.

"This your first hurricane?" Thomas asked.

"How'd you guess," said Vanessa with dry humor.

"Don't worry. Really. It doesn't get that bad here. It just sounds bad," he said, as the wind howled outside. "You want some coffee?"

That got her attention. "Real coffee?"

"Real coffee. I brought my little coffeemaker from home."

"You are a genius," she said. "And a hero. And—I will think of more compliments later. Where's the coffee?"

Coffee obtained, they settled in the back row of the theater, idly watching the other crew members entertain themselves down front.

"They wouldn't notice if the hurricane carried the both of us away," Vanessa said.

Thomas chuckled. He crossed and uncrossed his leg, then bounced his knee up and down as if they were in an earthquake, not a hurricane.

Vanessa, who must have noticed his nervous movement, asked if he was all right.

He stopped the nervous movement with an effort. "Me? Oh. Fine. I'm fine," he said. His flustered delivery belied his words. "Actually," he said, "I was thinking about the other day. In here." He leaned closer and lowered his voice. "On the stage."

"Ah," said Vanessa, in comprehension.

"But more importantly, I remember once—long ago—you promised to tell me more about yourself." He attempted a charming smile, to take her mind off his worries.

"Long ago," she echoed with a faint smile. "It certainly feels like it."

"Well, then," he said.

"I don't know," she said. "I have a question for you, actually."

"For me? Uh-oh."

"What, you got something to hide?" She elbowed him.

"Okay, okay. What's the question?"

"Have you ever thought about becoming a manager?"

Thomas whistled. "Wow, you don't beat around the bush, do you?"

"Not usually," she said.

"A serious question demands a serious answer. Let me think." He crossed his arms over his chest. "I don't know if I have a good answer for you. It's... not for me, Vanessa. I can't see myself as a manager."

"Why not?" she asked.

"You're not going to let me off the hook, are you? All right—for one thing, they wouldn't promote me to a manager position. How's that?"

"Let's say they would," she said.

"That's impossible."

"I think you're making excuses," said Vanessa.

Thomas winced as her words hit home like an arrow of truth. "Remind me never to get on your bad side," he said.

"What bad side?" Vanessa batted her eyelashes.

"Don't give me that innocent face," he said.

"You want to know what I really think?"

"God, no," he said, cradling his head in his hands and laughing.

"I think you would be a fantastic manager." She ticked off qualities on her fingers. "You're competent. You care about people. And you're a natural leader."

He sat up and rolled his eyes.

"Don't roll your eyes at me. You know I'm right."

"I'm flattered, is what I am," he said.

"I don't flatter."

Thomas sighed. "Fair enough. I yield. I'll ask Mr. Destiny for a manager job tomorrow."

"I could view your sarcasm as insubordination, you know." She wiggled her eyebrows at him.

"Take me away, officer—guilty as charged." He held out his wrists for imaginary handcuffs.

She encircled his wrists with her hands. "Busted!"

# Vanessa

The roar of the storm faded after midnight.

Vanessa turned over in her sleeping bag, unable to sleep.

She sat up.

The crew members by the front of the stage had finally tired themselves out after countless rounds of Twister, collapsing into sleeping bags strewn this way and that.

Thomas, behind the back row, appeared to be asleep.

Vanessa slid out of the sleeping bag and pulled a light jacket over her pajamas. She tiptoed to the lobby to get a view of the momentary calm.

She gazed out the window. Moonlight filtered down in patches as the clouds broke overhead.

*The eye of the storm.*

A noise behind her made her turn.

Thomas, barefoot, with tousled hair, gently closed the theater door behind him. "Is it the eye?" he asked, drowsiness making his voice husky.

She nodded and turned back to the window.

He came up behind her.

"Beautiful," he said.

He was close enough that if she leaned back, he would stop her fall.

"I'm going outside," she said.

She didn't look back to see if he followed her.

Outside, leaves covered the wet ground. The wind felt deceptively playful instead of fierce.

Vanessa turned in a slow circle in the plaza in front of American Dream. Though danger would return as soon as the opposite side of the eye drifted over, she felt fully alive, with every sense heightened.

She stopped turning and saw Thomas, silhouetted in shadow, leaning against one of the columns.

"Are you going to tell me to come inside?" she said as the clouds cast sprinkles of rain across the plaza.

"Why would I do that?" He left the shelter of the overhang and approached her, water beading on his hair.

"Your hair is all wet," she said. She reached out and touched a lock with one finger.

"So is yours," he retorted, tucking a damp curl behind her ear.

They stared each other down, blinking through the raindrops, getting more soaked by the moment, as if daring the other to be the first to give up and run for the building—until a flash of lightning broke the contest, sending them running back to the theater together.

## CHAPTER 12

*Vanessa*

Vanessa and Dirk took seats at the conference table inside the Mirror Castle meeting room.

Amy, the consultant, faced them across the table. Neat rows of folders lay within her reach, each color-coded and labeled by area.

"Vanessa," she said. "Dirk. So glad you could come. Let's get started, shall we?" Amy put down an expensive-looking pen and patted a nonexistent stray hair into place. "I heard from Mr. Destiny that the organizing committee has already revealed itself in Legacy. Is that so?"

Dirk, who appeared overawed by Amy and by the mere mention of Mr. Destiny, didn't speak.

Vanessa jumped in. "Yes, that's right."

"We have Paulina, Bob, Maribel, and"—she checked her notes—"Thomas, is that correct?"

"Yes," said Vanessa.

"Very good. So we have the pieces in place. But before we get to them, let's talk about you. How are you feeling about this process? Are there any concerns I can address? Any questions I can answer? If you are a little unsure about your role, I totally understand." Her voice dripped honey.

Vanessa shook her head and smiled at Amy. *If you think I'm that stupid, lady, you got another think coming.*

"I feel great about this," said Dirk. "I'm happy to be of service."

Amy took his remarks in stride. "Well, then, let's move on." She pulled out an elaborate chart. "These are all the Legacy employees. As you can see, they have a mark beside their names indicating their stance on the union. Plus sign if they lean toward management. Minus sign if they are against management. Question mark if their views are unknown." She handed the chart to Vanessa. "What we need you to do is update this list."

Vanessa handed the chart off to Dirk. "How do we do that, if we can't 'interrogate' anyone?"

"Every employee will receive a letter from Mr. Destiny with some interesting facts about the union. All you need to do is mention one of the facts. Perfectly legal. For example"—she turned to Dirk—"ask me if I knew the union could make me pay a penalty for not following the rules."

Dirk sat up straight, eager to roleplay. "Did you know," he said, "the union could make you pay a penalty for not following the rules?"

"No, I did not know that. Thank you for telling me! I will definitely not vote for the union," said Amy. "See? It's easy. And if they look uncomfortable, or argue—it's a minus." She tapped the chart with her pen. "As for the known troublemakers, they need to be carefully watched." Amy's cool gaze met Vanessa's carefully neutral one. "Do you know if any of the employees with minus signs have been found breaking company rules? Arriving late? Taking too long for breaks?"

Vanessa thought back to finding Thomas hidden behind the curtain, then pushed the thought out of her mind before it altered her expression. "I'm new here, so I don't know their histories. But I will take a closer look," she said.

"Please do," said Amy, emphasizing each word. "In addition, Mr. Destiny will be giving out a new award, called the Silver Mirror, to one attractions employee in each area. We will need you to select a suitable candidate for the award. Someone who follows all the rules. No troublemakers. Do you get my meaning? These will be given out before the vote."

Vanessa nodded.

She had to give them credit.

They'd thought of everything from carrot to stick.

And she would be expected to wield both.

## *Thomas*

Thomas tore open his pay envelope and found an extra sheet of paper tucked behind his measly check.

> *Dear Fellow Crew Member,*
>
> *You may have become aware of an outside organization attempting to infiltrate our workplace. As your friend, I would like to reassure you that your management team is hard at work to preserve the special relationship Destiny Park crew members currently enjoy with management. Did you know:*
>
> - *A union is a business that can't survive without taking money from your paycheck.*
> - *Union organizers will make salary and benefit promises to you they can't keep.*
> - *A union will control everything about your job and make it impossible to deal directly with your manager.*
>
> *Rest assured that we stand with you in this matter and do not wish to see an outside organization come between us. If you feel that we have done you wrong in the past, we ask you to give us a chance to make it right. If you have any concerns, please contact a member of management or call extension VOTENO (868366) from any house phone.*
>
> *Regards,*
> *John Destiny*

"Oh, now we're on a first-name basis, are we, 'John'? Bastard." Thomas shoved the envelope and letter into the nearest trash can, almost forgetting to remove his paycheck first. He stuffed the check in his pocket and stormed up to the Ghost Factory break room.

A new flyer hung from the bulletin board.

*Great. Just great. What now?*

The flyer, titled "The Silver Mirror: Reflecting Excellence," announced a new award for selected crew members in recognition of "Loyalty, Service, and Achievement," to be given on a date that coincidentally fell just before the union election.

*Of course.* His gaze shifted from the flyer to the sparkling new water cooler in the corner. *Now they're buttering us up. The question is: what will the knife be used for next?*

## Vanessa

After the meeting with the consultant, Vanessa retreated downstairs to the Legacy office. For once, hiding underground seemed like a peaceful alternative to being upstairs. She opened the door with a sigh of relief.

The open door permitted the unmistakable sound of weeping to reach her in the doorway.

Maribel sat in a second chair at Charlotte's desk. She attempted to compose herself as soon as she saw Vanessa. "I'm sorry," Maribel said to Charlotte. "I'll go."

"Maribel, what's wrong?" Vanessa rushed to her. "Are you okay?"

"I'm fine," Maribel sniffled. "Really. I'm sorry." She tried to stand up.

"You sit down," said Vanessa. She filled a cup with water and handed it to Maribel. "Now. Tell me what this is all about."

Charlotte and Maribel looked at each other. Charlotte shrugged as if to say, *It's up to you.*

Maribel wiped her eyes with a tissue. "It's just... people are saying... they're going to fire the union organizers. I can't... I can't lose my job. I didn't do anything wrong. I was just trying to make things better for us." Her tears threatened to spill.

Vanessa's blood ran cold. The consultant had just asked her to dig into her employees' records. Even a rumor of dismissal would make the crew uneasy, but an actual firing would terrify them into toeing the line. Even worse, she would be the one ordered to do the firing. How could she possibly comfort Maribel with reassurances that might turn out to be lies?

Vanessa kneeled next to Maribel's chair. "Maribel, listen to me. I have to be honest with you. This is all coming from much higher than me."

Tears rolled down Maribel's cheeks.

"But I promise: I only want to do right by you, and by all the crew members. I will do what I can. I wish I could offer more." Vanessa's heart ached at her own powerlessness.

"I know," said Maribel. "Thank you. I'm sorry I..."

Vanessa folded Maribel into a hug. "No apology necessary." She let go and stood up. "Are you off work now?"

Maribel nodded.

"Go home. Rest. Get your mind off things for a while, okay?" said Vanessa.

When Maribel had gone, Vanessa turned to Charlotte. "Where's Dirk?"

"He took those 'Silver Mirror' posters upstairs."

Vanessa whipped out her radio. "Legacy to Legacy 2."

"Legacy 2 here," Dirk's voice came over the radio.

"Legacy 2, what's your 20?"

"Outside Gold Rush."

"Stay where you are. I'm coming up. Legacy out." She clipped the radio back on her waistband. "I'm going to get to the bottom of this," she said to Charlotte.

"Good luck," said Charlotte.

Vanessa found Dirk at the Gold Rush overlook. "I got the posters up," he said.

"Can I see?"

"Sure." He led the way back to the Gold Rush break room.

Vanessa watched the faces of the crew members as they made their way deeper into the attraction building. She spotted far more frowns than usual.

When they reached the break room, Vanessa feigned interest in the poster, then turned to Dirk. "Did you notice something off with the crew today? They seem"—here she pretended to search for the right word, when in fact she had already planned out exactly what she was going to say—"nervous."

Dirk beamed. "You noticed."

*Good Lord, he's proud of himself.* "I did, yes. Why don't we take a little walk and you can tell me all about it?"

As they strolled through Legacy, Dirk explained that he'd taken the idea from Amy about "employees with minus signs" and run with it, dropping dire hints to the crew members as he went from attraction to attraction.

Vanessa's horror grew.

"Just enough to put the fear of God into them," he said. "Nothing we can get in trouble for."

She could tell he expected praise. "That shows a lot of initiative, Dirk." As they passed a vendor selling balloons, she added, "Maybe—to avoid any legal complications—run those ideas past me beforehand?" The strain of keeping a pleasant tone made her head pound.

"You got it," he said, making his fingers into guns and pointing them at her.

## Thomas

After work, Thomas slid into a booth at The Black Hole, the space-themed restaurant located in Galaxy. He squeezed a lemon wedge into his iced tea, then stirred it ferociously.

Paulina watched him over her soda.

Bob stared into his coffee.

"Where's Maribel?" said Thomas.

Paulina and Bob exchanged looks.

"You haven't heard?" said Paulina.

Thomas looked from Paulina to Bob. "What do you mean?"

"She went home crying," said Bob.

"What? Why?"

"Someone told her anyone involved with the union was going to get fired," said Bob.

Thomas swallowed iced tea the wrong way and coughed uncontrollably. "Who said that?" he choked out. "That's not even legal. That's a threat!"

"I don't know who said it," Bob replied. "I just know Maribel broke down in the office before she went home."

"This is not good," said Paulina.

"No kidding," said Thomas. "What are we going to do? They have everything on their side. Time. Money. Manpower. Access." He drank his tea. "What do we have? A handful of crew members trying to strategize in a cheeseburger joint. Honestly. It burns me up."

Galaxy chandeliers rotated slowly above them as they sat in silence.

"Have you"—Paulina hesitated before finishing her sentence—"talked to Vanessa?"

Thomas shot her a look.

"Just asking," Paulina said.

He sighed. "She's sympathetic, but her hands are tied. She can't do anything to help without jeopardizing her own job. And we're much better off with her than we would be without her."

"So, what are we going to do?" asked Bob.

"I don't think we should run scared. If anything," said Paulina, "they're scared, or they wouldn't be pulling out all the stops."

Thomas steepled his fingers, rested his chin on them, and closed his eyes. "Go on," he said.

"Think about it. They're throwing Jell-O at the wall and seeing what sticks. Why can't we turn that to our advantage? We need to take credit," she said. "For years, they refused to give us water coolers, and now look—a new water cooler in every attraction. Why's that, you ask? Just from mentioning the word 'union.'"

"And," Bob said, "imagine what could happen if we negotiated as a union."

Thomas's eyes flew open. "No matter what upper management does, it's just more proof that our union is powerful enough to make them react. And the more they react, the more they prove the point. People will start connecting the dots."

"It's still gonna get ugly," said Bob.

"No doubt," said Thomas. "But we can tell people that it's going to be ugly because management is running scared. It won't be a surprise. It might even bring a few fence-sitters over to our side."

"We need to write this up," said Paulina.

"I got this one," Thomas said. "Can you check on Maribel?" Paulina nodded.

"You all working the fireworks shift tomorrow?" said Bob.

"Not me," said Paulina. "I'm off."

"I'll be there," said Thomas.

They went their separate ways.

Instead of heading straight for the crew member parking lot, Thomas detoured to Galaxy's thrill ride, Escape Velocity, hoping it would shake the nerves out of him.

The attraction queue twisted and turned through dark inner hallways until it reached the loading platform lit with spotlights and neon.

He climbed into the two-person vehicle, pulled down the lap bar, and had just enough time to think *I wish Vanessa were here* before blasting off into the darkness.

# CHAPTER 13

## Vanessa

Vanessa crumpled up the second sheet of paper and dropped it in the trash can beside her desk. "Let's try this again," she said. "Please accept this letter—no."

She scratched it out.

"I would like to inform you—nope."

Another strike-through.

"I regret to inform you that I am officially resigning from my position as Legacy Area Manager." She sat back, cast a critical eye over the sentence, and decided that it would do.

She'd had enough.

Between Mr. Destiny, Dirk, and the union-busting consultant, she knew that sooner or later she would be asked to do something that didn't square with her sense of right and wrong. If that meant giving up her dream job at Destiny Park, so be it. She refused to be a party to underhanded dealings against people who were barely getting by despite working harder than Mr. Destiny ever had.

A wave of relief rolled over her as she finished writing the letter, followed by an ebb of regret when she slid the letter into a desk drawer.

## Thomas

The night sky stole over the Mirror Castle until every panel reflected the light of the moon.

Thomas, stationed at the border between Legacy and the Hub, waved a lit traffic control wand to keep visitors on the proper pathway away from the viewing area.

The lights in the trees twinkled through a range of color schemes, bright enough to be noticed, but too dim to make anything else visible in the darkness. Crew members around the Hub, sunk into darkness, were invisible but for their apparently disembodied wands.

The Hub filled with visitors. Most gravitated to the viewing area around the castle, but others planted themselves in the walkway and refused to budge.

Thomas, an old hand at crowd control, kept them moving with a mixture of cajoling and shouting, depending on the need of the moment and the politeness of the visitor in question.

He saw Vanessa's wand before he saw her. It floated all the way across the Legacy border at hip height until he recognized the person carrying it.

Vanessa looked lost.

"Vanessa!" he called.

She looked to him and smiled, changing direction to meet him.

"I didn't know you were coming tonight," he said. "Is this the first time you've seen the fireworks?"

"I didn't want to miss it," she said, standing beside him and attempting to wave her traffic wand in time with his.

"It's great!" His enthusiasm bubbled up from a sense of pride. Despite the stress of the job, he never forgot that he worked at the most beautiful theme park in the world. "You're going to love it." The night looked better than ever, with Vanessa's company and a spectacular show to enjoy.

He noticed her smile slip. *She must be tired from working later than usual.* He redoubled his efforts to bring a smile to her face, clowning with the traffic wand and dancing to the ambient music much to the delight of the nearby visitors.

Her smile, though it came more frequently, turned more melancholy by the minute.

The fanfare rippled over the sound system, announcing the beginning of the show. Points of light shot into the sky.

Thomas cheered along with the rest of the crowd. He turned to catch Vanessa's expression.

She patted her sleeve against each eye and continued watching the fireworks.

"Are you okay?" he shouted over the explosions and the roar of the music.

"I'm fine," she shouted back.

He looked closer.

Her lip trembled.

"No, you're not. What's wrong?" It really was awkward to shout.

She motioned him closer. "I can't stay," she said.

"It's only a couple minutes longer; are you sure?" he asked, assuming she meant the fireworks show.

"No! Not the show. Here. I have to go. I'm resigning."

A huge firework exploded overhead and the sound reverberated in Thomas's chest. His lips parted in shock. "Why?"

"I can't do this. I can't do the things they're going to ask me to do. For God's sake, Thomas, they're probably going to make me fire some innocent crew member."

"You don't know that," he pleaded.

She shook her head. "I can't do it."

A white star exploded, followed by a ringed planet.

He ran one hand through his hair and gripped it as if he would pull it out by the roots. *Think, Thomas, think!*

"Vanessa, listen, I know this is impossible. I know you are in a terrible position and I don't fault you for wanting out. But, please, I know we are so much better off with you here than with anyone else."

The fireworks flashed in their eyes as his gaze met hers.

"I—" Vanessa began, then whirled away into the crowd, which closed behind her as she made her way through. She was lost to sight within seconds.

The last firework faded away with a fluttering hiss.

# CHAPTER 14

## Vanessa

The park emptied rapidly after the fireworks show, leaving her little cover as the crowd thinned. Vanessa fled the Hub and veered into Discovery, hoping no one would recognize her there. Most of the shops and restaurants had already closed.

She found the front entrance to the Coffee Garden locked, but a gap in the wall of living bamboo gave access to the outdoor garden adjacent to the building. Vanessa climbed through and collapsed on a padded outdoor bench.

*No one will bother me here.*

The thought contained relief and despair in equal measure.

Exhausted, she stretched out full length, laid her head on her arms, and closed her eyes.

Her thoughts echoed without cease until—without intending to—she drifted off to sleep.

She woke to the sound of leaf blowers.

Had she fallen asleep outside?

Why was she snuggling a traffic wand?

Disoriented, she rubbed her eyes to clear her vision. A glance at the sky, visible above the bamboo, revealed a pale hint of the rising sun.

Vanessa stood up and attempted to tug her clothing into a semblance of respectability.

It was hopeless.

Tucking the traffic wand under her arm, she climbed through the bamboo gap the same way she came in.

Along the street, landscapers busily replanted flowers under the glare of floodlights. No one paid her any mind as she groggily made her way back to Legacy and downstairs to the office.

She unlocked the door and switched on the lights, then dropped the traffic wand on the counter and fired up the coffee machine. While it brewed, she retrieved her purse and went to the ladies' room to splash water on her face and apply a little hand cream, lipstick, and pressed powder.

None of her efforts removed the creases stamped into her cheek by the bench pad.

Back in the office, she sat down with the first of several cups of coffee, then pulled her resignation letter out and laid it on her desk.

By the time she heard the office door open, heralding Charlotte's arrival, she had polished the letter to her satisfaction.

Charlotte poked her head into Vanessa's office. "What are you doing here so early?"

"I had to get some work done," said Vanessa.

Charlotte peered at her. "Isn't that the same outfit you had on yesterday?"

"This?" said Vanessa, looking down at herself as if this was the first time she'd noticed anything amiss. "I suppose it is."

"What did you do last night? Did you go out?" Her eyes widened. "Were you on a date?"

"No! No dates. Just a late night," Vanessa explained.

"What are you working on this early in the morning?"

Vanessa panicked and turned the letter facedown on her desk. "Nothing."

"Nothing," repeated Charlotte, eyeing the paper. "All right, you don't have to tell me anything." She walked away slowly. "I just work here."

"Wait," said Vanessa. "Come back."

Charlotte came back so fast she nearly skidded into Vanessa's office.

"Sit down," said Vanessa.

Charlotte sat.

"I don't know how to say this, but... I'm leaving, Charlotte."

"You're what now?"

"I'm leaving," said Vanessa.

"You're leaving? As in on a jet plane?"

"More or less."

Charlotte blew out her breath and leaned back in her chair. She broke eye contact with Vanessa and examined her nails instead. "Really."

Vanessa didn't know what to say to that.

Charlotte continued, still refusing to look at Vanessa. "So that's it, then. You're gonna waltz right on out of here?"

"I don't know if that's how I would—" Vanessa started.

"How you would put it?" finished Charlotte. "You want to know how I would put it?"

Floored, Vanessa simply gestured for Charlotte to continue.

"You're the one who told Maribel you'd do your best to be there for her, and now you're walking out when things get hot?"

"Charlotte, for all I know"—Vanessa got up, shut the door, sat down, and lowered her voice—"they'll make me the one who has to do the firing. Isn't that worse?"

Charlotte shook her head. "All these people want to do is make a choice without interference. Do they want a union? Do they not want a union? Who knows?" Charlotte threw up her hands. "But it's not a fair choice when management is throwing everything at them from threats to free t-shirts."

"I know that," Vanessa said, lifting her chin indignantly. "You know what else I know?"

Charlotte crossed her arms.

"I know you were copying those names and addresses for the organizing committee. I also know the company was legally required to give the organizers that information as soon as the campaign became official. So I asked myself, 'Why would Charlotte need to do it secretly?'"

Charlotte stared at the ceiling as if she were looking for leaks.

"And you know what? I did my homework and found out the company gave the organizers a pile of useless paper, full of missing information. So you did what you could to help, and I pretended I didn't see it." Vanessa placed both hands on her desk for emphasis. "You think I don't want people to make a choice? You're wrong. I've been fighting to protect that choice since the get-go."

Charlotte uncrossed her arms and leaned forward. "Then why are you giving up the fight?"

"Because I can't win. At this point I can only hurt people."

"You're wrong. At this point you might be the only one left to defend them."

They glared at each other.

"I have to get some work done," said Charlotte. She stood up and stalked out, slamming the door behind her.

# Thomas

Thomas, bleary-eyed and fatigued, blessed his stars for landing him at Ghost Factory for the day. The dark interior soothed him, and the visitors found their experience enhanced rather than diminished by his sleep-deprived scowl.

From his station at the unload area, he had only to keep an eye on the visitors exiting the carriage vehicles. He tread the moving walkway on automatic pilot, placing one foot in front of the other without having to think about it.

Instead, he thought about the previous night.

After the fireworks show, he had completed his tasks and stowed away his traffic wand before setting off in a futile search for Vanessa. He'd known it would be almost impossible to track her down if she stayed upstairs in the park, but that didn't stop him from walking through Legacy, Fantasy, Galaxy, and Discovery just in case, before giving up outside the Coffee Garden and heading home much later than usual.

He made a mental note to get a large coffee from the cafe on his next break.

In a way, he was glad he hadn't found her. He wanted to offer comfort, but he would have died rather than have her feel pressured. He firmly believed that she should do whatever was best for her, and could only hope it would coincide with his fervent wish that she would stay.

Would she miss the Halloween party? Thomas hoped not. He'd agonized over his costume until—at last—it had finally come together in a way that made him anticipate the party even more.

## CHAPTER 15

*Vanessa*

On the day of the party, Vanessa locked her office and slung a heavier-than-usual bag over her shoulder. "I'm going to get ready," she told Charlotte, whose manner had been cool since they clashed over Vanessa's plan to resign.

Charlotte didn't look up. "Suit yourself," she said.

At the costume department, Vanessa retrieved an armful of clothing from the pickup window and carried it into the women's locker room.

Piece by piece, she traded her clothing for a crew member costume: slacks, shirt, jacket, and finally a wide-brimmed felt hat.

A red neckerchief remained on the bench.

She dug in her bag for the pair of scissors she'd packed. Careful not to cut the knot itself, she sliced through the fabric next to the knot, cutting all the way through to the other side. She reached into her bag again, this time for a portable sewing kit and a bit of Velcro.

Vanessa stitched one piece of Velcro to the back of the knot, and the other to the cut end, adding a few extra stitches to keep the fabric from unraveling and the knot from untying.

Without removing her hat, she swung the knotted end around her shoulder to meet the other end and pressed the Velcro tabs together.

*Voila.*

At the mirror, she examined her handiwork and smiled. A touch of blush and a swipe of lipstick made her feel fully armored.

On the walk back to the Legacy office, she carried her head higher. Her spine straightened and her steps rang down the corridor. She reached up to tilt the hat just so before opening the office door.

This time, Charlotte looked up, disbelief written across her face. "You're wearing … that?"

"Yup," said Vanessa, breezing past Charlotte into her own office, where she pulled open a drawer and retrieved her letter of resignation.

She turned on the office shredder behind Charlotte's desk and fed the letter through with a sigh of satisfaction.

"Did you just … ?" said Charlotte.

"Yes ma'am, I did."

"You're going to fight the good fight!" said Charlotte. She punched Vanessa playfully on the shoulder.

"Ow," said Vanessa, wincing and laughing at the same time. "I'm sure going to try."

## Thomas

In the men's locker room, Thomas pulled out the items he'd carefully hung up in his locker earlier that day. Tonight, he would forego a traditional Halloween costume in favor of something more refined.

He discarded his Ghost Factory shirt for a lightly patterned silver-gray long-sleeved dress shirt. He shook out a pair of finely woven black slacks before slipping them on, neatly tucking the shirt into the pants. He added a supple leather belt, soft dress socks, and leather dress shoes, followed by a handsome waistcoat to match the slacks.

For the final sartorial touch, he carefully tied a black silk necktie with an elegant knot.

His costume remained incomplete without one crucial, signifying accessory. He reached into his locker, pulled out the radio he'd borrowed from Ghost Factory, and clipped it to his belt.

Thomas checked his appearance in the full-length mirror. *Nice.*

The spring in his step propelled him up and out into the park. The setting sun gilded the nearby buildings with light. In such a glorious setting it was difficult not to be optimistic for the future.

He followed the Legacy Halloween party signs through Discovery to Aquaverse, then bounded up the stairs to the double doors of the Aquarium Room.

Thomas pushed open the doors and walked through a row of giant sea fans studded with tiny blue bulbs. Their undulating light reflected on a transparent acrylic piano in the center of the room, its keys depressed by an unseen hand as it automatically played a delicate melody.

A table stood nearby, piled high with seafood of every kind: lobster tails, stone crab claws, and oysters on ice; towering displays of crab legs; peel-and-eat shrimp; and bowls of crab ceviche. A separate table displayed tiers of key lime pie, cheesecake, and petit fours.

Thomas spotted Charlotte at the bar. She noticed him and raised her glass of champagne in greeting.

"This is something else," said Thomas as he signaled the bartender.

Charlotte sipped from her glass. "Enough to make you vote no on the union?"

Thomas laughed. "Hardly. But I'll happily enjoy the attempt at bribery."

He collected his own glass of champagne and they moved to the buffet.

Thomas had picked up a plate and was piling it high with every available crustacean when he noticed Charlotte staring over his shoulder.

"I'll catch you later," Charlotte said. She glided away.

Thomas turned around to see what Charlotte had been looking at.

It was Vanessa, dressed head to toe in the Gold Rush costume. She smiled at him from across the room.

She walked toward him.

Suddenly, he wished he wasn't carrying several pounds of seafood. He hastily set down the plate and tried to be subtle about brushing off his hands.

"Thomas," she said, almost solemn, but with a hint of mischief in her eye.

"Vanessa," he replied. "I like your choice of costume. You look like one of us."

"Thank you," said Vanessa. "And is that a radio I spy on your hip?" She took one step back and looked him up and down.

He awaited her verdict.

"You're dressed as a manager!" she said.

"Happy Halloween," said Thomas, and raised his glass to her.

"Happy Halloween," said Vanessa. She reached out near his shoulder and felt the shirtsleeve fabric between her thumb and forefinger. "It's beautiful. I would toast you, but I haven't hit the bar yet."

"Can I get you something?" he asked. He leaned in and spoke quietly. "My treat. For a farewell toast?"

"About that," she said. Vanessa drew him aside near the aquarium. "I changed my mind. I'm staying."

He wanted to hug her. He wanted to grab her hands and spin in circles like children until they both fell down, dizzy and laughing. Instead, he let his joy shine forth in a smile that crinkled the corners of his eyes. "That's wonderful news. A celebratory toast is much better than a farewell toast, anyway."

"I couldn't agree more. I will have to give you a raincheck for later, though—for now, I must mingle. And you have a plate of seafood to get back to, I think."

# Vanessa

Vanessa moved through the crowd, greeting crew members and admiring costumes, until she became too hungry to abstain from the buffet any longer.

*It's my turn to pile up a plate.*

Fully provisioned, she found Charlotte's table and sat down. She complimented Charlotte's radiant green sequined cocktail dress, then fell to cracking crab legs with a practiced hand.

They chatted amiably, back on solid ground after their temporary falling-out.

Across the room, Thomas appeared to be telling a story that involved balancing on one leg and gesturing wildly.

Charlotte followed Vanessa's gaze. "You're staring," she said.

Vanessa choked on her drink.

Charlotte laughed. "Vanessa, you are too easy to rile."

"I am not," Vanessa protested. "Besides, this is Destiny Park, not 'The Dating Game.'"

"Could've fooled me," said Charlotte.

"What are you doing with your art lately, Charlotte?"

"I see you changing the subject. But I'll let you do it because I love to talk about myself."

"Please do," said Vanessa, with a flourish of her hand.

"I am still working on my portfolio. Someday—when it's ready—I'll submit it to the design department, see if I can get on the art team."

"Don't stop," said Vanessa. "I'm rooting for you."

"Thank you," said Charlotte.

Maribel approached the table. "Is this seat taken?"

"No! By all means, have a seat," said Vanessa. "I love your witch costume."

"Thank you," said Maribel. She set her plate and glass on the table, removed her pointed hat, and sat down.

"That reminds me," said Vanessa. "I have something to show you. Grab my neckerchief."

Maribel looked at Vanessa like she'd gone mad.

"I haven't lost my mind. Yet. I promise. Go on, give it a pull."

Maribel reached toward Vanessa, seized the fabric, and tugged on it.

It came away in Maribel's hand. She laughed. "What'd you do?" she said.

"I altered this one. It's a prototype," Vanessa said.

"I like it," said Maribel. "Now you just have to get Mr. Destiny on board."

The three women settled into pleasant conversation punctuated by occasional refills of their glasses and plates.

"Oh, my," said Vanessa, staring past Charlotte.

"What?" said Charlotte. She whipped around to see what Vanessa was looking at.

Dirk marched through the rows of sea fans, dressed like a Prussian nobleman, complete with dress military jacket, gold epaulets, a sash, and a crown.

Crew members were already crowding around to admire his choice of costume, blocking Vanessa's view.

"Excuse me," she said to Charlotte and Maribel. "I'll be back." She pushed back her chair and stood up, determined to greet Dirk and take a closer look at his Halloween get-up.

"Are you a ... prince?" Vanessa said, joining the crowd that had formed around Dirk.

"Prince Dirk, at your service." He bowed stiffly, from the waist.

"That's quite a costume," Vanessa said. It was so over the top that she almost found it endearing, in a weird way, despite her dislike for him. He seemed genuinely happy for the first time.

She withdrew from the group and took a turn about the room, soaking in the beauty of the undersea-themed lighting and the flashes of silver from the fish in the aquarium. The sound of the self-playing piano mingled with the chatter of crew members and the clink of glasses and silver.

As the night progressed, enough of the crew members partook of the cash bar to loosen their inhibitions. Laughter grew loud and stories more outlandish as Vanessa circulated through the crowd.

A commotion in the center of the floor drew her attention. Someone figured out how to shut off the piano, and someone sat down to play.

The crowd cheered as Dirk launched into a spirited performance.

Vanessa watched from a distance. Absorbed in the strange spectacle, she didn't notice Thomas standing quietly next to her until she caught the scent of pine.

"I didn't know he could play," said Vanessa.

"He's talented," said Thomas.

Side by side, they listened to the music for the length of a song.

"I haven't forgotten that toast you promised me," said Vanessa.

"I would never dream of disappointing you," said Thomas. "Would you like to catch a little fresh air?"

Vanessa nodded. "Sounds refreshing," she said.

"See that side door over there? Past the dessert table? If you go out that door, there's a little fire escape that overlooks the park. You can take a breather while I fetch the glasses," Thomas said.

They parted. Vanessa found the stairs just as Thomas described. She sat down on the top stair. The view of the border between Discovery and Galaxy contained layers of natural beauty topped with the glowing globes and spokes of a space-themed Ferris wheel.

The door behind her clicked open.

Thomas emerged from inside, carrying two champagne flutes filled with ruby red liquid. He handed one to her and sat down on the same stair.

"It's a champagne–pomegranate cocktail," he said. "Specialty of the night. Champagne, or something like it, with pomegranate juice, and some of those little pomegranate seeds floating on top."

"Arils," Vanessa said, holding her glass up to the light and turning it back and forth.

"Arils, right. I can never remember that."

"So what should we toast to?" She glanced over at him and felt little butterflies take wing in her stomach.

He pondered the question. "How about, 'To new beginnings,'?"

"'To new beginnings.' I like the sound of that. I feel like we should add something to make it more martial, though."

"Martial?"

"You know. More warlike," she said.

"We could toast like Vikings," he said. "They were very into war."

Vanessa laughed. "Okay, to new beginnings, but like the Vikings. How do we do that?"

"Face me."

They scooted around to face each other.

"Put your glass down for a second. Now we link arms"—he crooked his arm in front of him and she hooked her arm through it—"and you put your glass back into your hand like this."

They both giggled as they awkwardly maneuvered their glasses into place.

"To new beginnings," he said.

"To new beginnings."

A toast begun in jest turned intimate as they tipped their glasses back simultaneously.

"I think I drank an aril," he said as they untangled their arms.

"I think I did too," she said.

They smiled at each other.

---

The crowd thinned as the night wound to a close. One by one—or, in some cases, two by two—the crew members departed, leaving behind only the venue staff and the two Legacy managers.

Vanessa had no idea how to get Dirk to go home.

He sat at the piano, with a score of empty wine glasses perched on its acrylic ledge, singing softly and accompanying himself with a sad melody. Despite his obvious state, he didn't miss a note.

"Dirk..." Vanessa patted his epauletted shoulder. "Dirk. You should go home now."

He stopped singing, at least. The piano melody continued.

She tried again. "Dirk. Let me call you a cab."

He mashed a discordant batch of notes all at once, then crossed his arms on the piano and dropped his head on his arms with a thud.

Vanessa pulled at his shoulders to make him sit up.

"All I ever wanted was to work here. But I'll never be a manager."

As he spoke, Vanessa's eyes widened more and more. "Dirk, I'm sure you—"

"No, I won't," he interrupted. "I'm not stupid. I thought"—he picked up an empty wine glass and studied it—"I thought if I did everything they wanted they would finally see I could be one of them."

"What did they want exactly?" asked Vanessa, alarmed, but Dirk didn't pay any attention.

"They were just using me," he said. He threw the plastic wine glass to the floor.

Vanessa slid onto the piano bench and patted his shoulder again.

Dirk reeked of alcohol.

"Mr. Destiny wants me to talk about all the crew members," he said, wiping his reddened eyes. "I'm supposed to blab on the same people who bought me drinks and made me a tip jar—a tip jar!" He held up another wine glass, this one stuffed with moist dollar bills. "And for what? He's not ever going to make me a manager. At least the crew thought I was fun. No one ever thinks I'm fun. I know what they think of me."

Vanessa held her tongue. Whatever he needed to say, he needed to say it—no matter how confused it came out.

"I may be Dirk the Jerk, but I'm not his jerk. I'm my own jerk," he concluded before slumping over the piano again.

"Dirk?"

He flopped his head up and down.

She took it as encouragement. "You can be whatever you want, starting tomorrow. You need—as someone very wise once told me—to fight the good fight." She hauled him to his feet and steered him toward the door. "It's time for a new beginning."

## CHAPTER 16

*Vanessa*

"Buck up, soldier," Vanessa said as she handed Dirk a mug of strong coffee. She sat down at her desk with her own mug.

Dirk drank the scalding hot coffee and winced.

Vanessa blew on her coffee and observed him. His gelled hair sat askew over his puffy eyes. She pulled a wad of dollars out of her purse and laid it on her desk. It smelled of wine.

Dirk eyed the pile. "Is that…?"

"Your 'tips' from last night, yes," said Vanessa.

He scooped up the bills and blushed. "I remember playing the piano."

"Anything else?"

He shook his head slowly. "Was there something else?" he asked.

She had to walk the line between magnanimous and menacing, well enough that he would believe she had something on him but chose not to use it. She let the silence play before she answered. "I don't think it's anything we need to address right now."

He met her gaze with panic in his eyes.

*Bingo.*

"You performed beautifully, by the way," she said, letting him off the hook just a little.

"Thank you," he said.

"Did you know there's an opening for a piano player at the Galaxy Lounge?" she asked.

"No kidding?" He laughed nervously.

Vanessa nodded and sipped her coffee. "You know, we still need to pick someone for the Silver Mirror award."

He opened his mouth to speak, checked himself, and subsided.

"Did you have someone in mind?" she said.

"I was just thinking about Marco. He's perfect. He's so new he hasn't done anything wrong," Dirk said.

Coming from Dirk, it was a shockingly good choice. On paper, Marco fulfilled the union-buster's requirement—no "troublemakers"—but in reality, it would rile the crew members to have someone so new selected for a special prize.

The Silver Mirror ploy would backfire on upper management, and they'd never see it coming.

Now Dirk was watching her with his eyebrows raised as if he were trying to communicate something without saying it.

Was he intentionally trying to tank the true purpose of the award?

Did he think she would let his inebriated scene slide if he did?

There was no way to know.

Regardless, she couldn't look a gift horse in the mouth. If he wanted to ally himself with her—even temporarily—she wouldn't stop him.

She needed all the help she could get.

## Thomas

The underground radio blared from the overhead speakers as Thomas dug a handful of leaflets out of his locker.

"Attention all crew members. You're listening to The Voice of Destiny..."

"I'm trying not to," Thomas muttered.

"...your number one source of information on all things Destiny Park. The park will be open today from 9:00 a.m. to 6:00 p.m., and the parade will step off promptly at 3:00 p.m. Don't forget to pick up your free t-shirt in the main corridor during park hours. Park management respectfully requests that you report all unauthorized third-party organization activity immediately to a manager so that we can preserve our workplace harmony."

Thomas snorted as he slammed his locker shut.

"Thank you, and we hope that you'll continue to find your Destiny today!"

The radio station blessedly returned to Top 40 programming.

Thomas glanced down the aisle. Finding no one in sight, he quickly slipped a folded pamphlet into the slot of each locker in the row. Distributing union literature off the clock was completely legal, but it only took one unfriendly observer to go running off to management to stir up trouble.

He turned a corner and saw Bob head down a row with a handful of pamphlets. Thomas pivoted to the opposite direction and worked his way down another aisle.

By the time they ran out, they'd leafleted almost every locker in the men's locker room. Thomas and Bob exchanged a silent nod and headed to separate exits.

When Thomas emerged, he spotted Maribel coming out of the women's locker room.

She, too, nodded at him before striding off.

*Mission accomplished, almost.* Thomas patted his pocket as he walked, confirming he'd held on to one of the leaflets.

In the Ghost Factory break room, he smoothed out the paper. Bob and Maribel, he knew, would pin their last copies in American Dream and Gold Rush. He read it over one more time as he pushed pins through the paper and into the bulletin board.

The leaflet, written after their desperate meeting in The Black Hole, predicted that Destiny Park management would continue to apply pressure (such as letters, meetings, and radio broadcasts) along with bribery (like parties, prizes, and free t-shirts) in an attempt to sway the crew members to vote against unionizing. Thomas had taken pains to point out that management's reaction to the fledgling union only proved how powerful a union could be.

Every attempt to bust the union, positive or negative, would make the point all over again. The letter closed with the usual plea to "Vote yes!"

Win or lose, he wasn't going down without a fight.

## CHAPTER 17

*Vanessa*

The Mirror Castle loomed over Vanessa. She had received a personal summons to meet with Amy, the consultant, prior to awarding the Silver Mirror.

Vanessa squared her shoulders and pressed the button of the now-familiar elevator that would carry her to the executive offices.

Upon entering Mr. Destiny's office, she found Amy behind the desk.

Mr. Destiny, as was often the case, had somewhere else to be.

"Good afternoon," said Amy.

"Good afternoon," said Vanessa.

Amy picked up one of the awards from the credenza and handed it to Vanessa. "Here you go. We'll be bringing along a photographer, of course, to record the occasion."

"We?" said Vanessa, examining the Silver Mirror. The shiny award, heavy in her hands, was already covered in fingerprints.

"Oh, yes. I'm coming with you to help out."

"I'm sure I'll be fine," said Vanessa. Her smile showed her teeth.

"Nonsense. That's what I'm here for—to make sure things go the way they're supposed to," Amy replied.

"Great!" said Vanessa, which was not how she felt at all.

"Your secretary said Marco was scheduled to work the parade this afternoon?"

"That's right," said Vanessa. "They should be wrapping up shortly."

"Perfect. We'll have the other parade crew members to witness the award."

The door opened, and a man with an elaborate camera rig entered.

"And there's our photographer. Let's get this show on the road," said Amy.

The three of them walked to American Dream to intercept the parade crew.

Vanessa figured that if Amy wanted so badly to be in charge, Amy could take the blame if anything went wrong. She resolved to stay in the background as much as possible.

"Which one is Marco?" Amy whispered when they arrived.

"The one with the Marco nametag," said Vanessa.

She handed the award to Amy.

"Congratulations, Marco," Amy said loudly, as if Marco were hard of hearing. "You've been selected to receive the Silver Mirror award for your loyalty, service, and achievement."

The other crew members gathered around as the photographer snapped pictures indiscriminately.

Marco—polite, amiable Marco who had danced with her at the carriage wash—looked to Vanessa with confusion written across his face. He knew as well as she did that he didn't deserve an award.

Vanessa felt a surge of guilt for putting him in an uncomfortable position.

"Why don't we all take a nice picture?" said Amy.

Only a few crew members shuffled toward Marco.

Amy stood back and attempted to herd all the crew members into the shot by waving her arms. "You, get in the back. You, move over. You, move to the front. Not there. There!" When that wasn't enough to get the effect she was looking for, she charged forward with the Silver Mirror in her hand.

Vanessa delicately turned one foot out.

Amy caught her high heel on Vanessa's shoe and lost her grip on the Silver Mirror. Her forward momentum launched the award end over end, sparkling in the sun, until it fell and exploded in a thousand shards on the concrete.

The crew members scattered, dodging the broken mirror shards and laughing.

Amy's face turned bright red.

Marco looked relieved.

Vanessa calmly unclipped her radio and called for help with the cleanup.

## Thomas

When Thomas heard Vanessa's voice, he snatched up the radio from its charging station at the Ghost Factory loading area and held it to his ear.

"Legacy to Janitorial," she said.

"Janitorial here."

"Janitorial, we need a glass cleanup in front of American Dream."

"Copy that, Legacy. We'll send someone up."

"A glass cleanup?" Thomas mused aloud. He got Paulina's attention at the other loading area position. "Did you hear that?"

"What?" said Paulina.

"A glass cleanup outside American Dream."

Paulina made a confused face. "Why would they need to clean up glass outside? Did someone break a window?"

They continued loading visitors into the carriages.

A few minutes later, Paulina's friends Laura and Claudia returned from the parade. They bustled into the loading area clearly brimming with a story to tell.

"What happened at the parade?" asked Thomas.

"Well," said Claudia, swishing her blonde hair over her shoulder, "some lady came down to the parade to give Marco one of those new awards."

Laura picked up the thread of the story. "Marco was supposed to have his picture taken with the trophy, but she wanted everyone to get in the picture."

"Nobody wanted to get in the picture, though, so she started waving her hands around like crazy to make people move, and somehow she tripped," said Claudia.

"And the trophy went flying and smashed into a million pieces!" Laura finished.

Paulina and Thomas exchanged a look.

"Who else was there?" said Thomas.

"Oh, Vanessa and some photographer guy," said Claudia.

"So nobody got the award," Thomas said.

"Not unless they swept it up and put it in a bag to take home," said Laura. She burst into giggles. "So much for the Silver Mirror!"

# CHAPTER 18

## Vanessa

The Legacy office door shot open, and in walked Mr. Destiny. Seeing Mr. Destiny in the Legacy office was like spotting a bear in your backyard: fascinating, but also frightening.

Vanessa took a step backward as he charged into the room.

"Office. Now," he said, barely breaking stride as he barreled past her into her office.

She followed him. "Mr. Destiny, is everything okay?"

"Shut the door," he said.

She complied.

He seated himself in her chair, forcing her to sit in one of the guest chairs.

"I've come to a conclusion," he said. "We need to send a message that Destiny Park will not tolerate those who continue to break the rules."

"I'm not sure I follow, sir," said Vanessa. Her heartbeat increased.

"Take your crew member Paulina, for example." He pulled a paper out of his pocket and unfolded it. "Did you know that Paulina has been late no less than 4 times in the last month? And—look at this—Maribel has called in sick far more than the average crew member." He tapped the paper.

"Then we have Robert," he said.

"Robert? You mean Bob?"

"Yes, Bob, whatever," said Mr. Destiny.

"Which one?" said Vanessa. She didn't dare ask him if he meant Short Bob or Tall Bob.

"There's more than one?" Mr. Destiny rolled his eyes. "The one who keeps taking extra breaks to eat yogurt."

Vanessa raised her eyebrows. "Really?"

"I have it on good information. And then there's Thomas, your trainer."

Vanessa felt a blush develop on her cheeks.

Thankfully, Mr. Destiny didn't notice. He continued his rant. "Thomas is not training the new hires sufficiently."

*That's all they could come up with?*

"I would be happy to speak with them to correct these issues," said Vanessa, knowing full well the conversation was not headed in that direction.

"For some of them, yes. But the other crew members won't take it seriously unless there are real consequences."

*Oh, no. Please don't.*

"So pick one. Let 'em go," he said.

Vanessa felt like a trap door had opened under her feet. "You know those are the four crew members on the organizing committee." It was a statement, not a question.

Mr. Destiny stared her down. "Totally unrelated."

"It doesn't look unrelated," Vanessa said.

He shrugged. "It would look related if we fired all of them. Hypothetically speaking. Which we're not." He stood up. "Do it before the vote. Let me know when it's done." He left Vanessa alone in her office.

Her thoughts tumbled over each other. Had she erred by not broadcasting enough enthusiasm for busting the union? Did the shattered Silver Mirror tip him over the edge to pure retaliation?

Or had he just decided to pull out all the stops in his hellbent attempt to stop the crew members from unionizing?

She'd tried so hard to keep everything in balance, and she'd failed.

How on earth could she select someone to fire when none of them deserved to be fired?

Quitting wouldn't save anyone. They'd just find someone else to wield the ax.

Anger boiled up within her. The injustice of it all! Vanessa shot out of her seat and nearly knocked over the chair. Her hands tingled as she reached for the schedule binder.

*Thomas. Thomas, where are you?* She flipped the pages until she found him. *American Dream.* She did her best to compose herself before exiting the office. The spread of panic and rumors wouldn't help her or her crew members.

Vanessa entered American Dream through the back. The show played in the dimly lit theater, making her pause to give her eyes time to adjust to the darkness.

She spotted Thomas in the audience and sat down next to him. "We need to talk," she said. "Privately."

Thomas checked his watch. "I'm on lunch at 12:00. Can you get free?"

"Yes, but where can we meet?"

Thomas considered. "Ride Ghost Factory just before 12:00. I'll make sure Paulina's at the unloading station and I'll meet you when you get off the ride. No one but Paulina will see us. Then we can go somewhere private to talk."

The show was coming to an end, leaving them only seconds before the lights came up, but she couldn't help wondering where he had in mind.

"Where is it?" asked Vanessa.

"It's... hard to explain. You'll understand when you see it," said Thomas.

Vanessa stood up and hurried to the exit with the American Dream finale echoing behind her.

She spent the remainder of the morning in her office, poring over the "Union-Free Toolbox" and "Union-Free for You and Me" in hopes of discovering a way out of her terrible conundrum.

A close reading of the text produced no obvious answers, but it did unearth a sliver of hope. One passage revealed that a terminated employee could appeal to an independent labor board for reinstatement if he or she believed the termination was a result of legally protected union organizing activities. Since the chapter was written with a union-busting slant, it focused on how to avoid run-ins with the labor board—but the information was helpful all the same.

A glance at the clock revealed the nearness of the noon hour. Vanessa reshelved the handbooks and set out for Ghost Factory.

## Thomas

Thomas smoothed his Ghost Factory waistcoat and brushed off the shoulders of his jacket, then shoved his hands into his pockets in an attempt to stop fidgeting.

"Are you okay?" asked Paulina.

"Oh, yeah," said Thomas. He stared at the never-ending stream of carriages, hoping with the approach of each trundling ride vehicle that Vanessa would emerge at last.

He caught a flash of red hair from an approaching carriage.

It was Vanessa. She stepped onto the moving walkway, which carried her to Thomas and Paulina at the end of the unloading area.

"This way," said Thomas.

He escorted her behind a barrier parallel to the walkway and along a brick wall to a door hidden in a dark corner of the unloading area. Thomas opened it. "Stairs. Watch your step," he said.

After closing the door behind them, he followed her down the steep staircase. They stood face to face in a long room—more like a dead-end hallway—lined with abandoned mechanical figures.

"What is this place?" she said.

"Storage. They put spare or broken mechanical figures in here." He patted the disembodied head of a ghost horse.

"Festive," said Vanessa.

"But private," said Thomas. "If a bit claustrophobic. So, what's wrong? How can I help?"

Vanessa rubbed her forehead. "I don't know how to make this sound any better than it is, so I'm just going to say it straight out."

"Go ahead," said Thomas. "I'm listening."

"Mr. Destiny ordered me to fire one of the Legacy organizers."

"Which one?"

"That's just it," said Vanessa. "He doesn't care. 'Pick one,' he said." Vanessa looked disgusted. "What am I supposed to do?"

"Did he say why? Like, explicitly?" asked Thomas.

"He made up some garbage about what you all did wrong—nothing to do with unionizing, of course—and when I called him on it he gave me some mealy-mouthed response. I know he's just trying to frighten the crew members into voting 'no,' but there's nothing I can do about it."

The desperation in her voice tore through him. "If someone is wrongfully fired for organizing, they can appeal to get their job back," he said.

"I know," she said. "But that's not a guarantee. And it doesn't prevent the other crew members from getting scared off the whole idea of a union. One termination could be all it takes to torpedo everything you've done."

"Maybe not," said Thomas. "What if... what if you fired someone like he wants you to, but the crew members think you did it for a legitimate reason?"

"That doesn't make any sense," said Vanessa.

"Mr. Destiny wants you to fire a union organizer to send a message, right?"

"Right," said Vanessa.

"Well, what if you fire someone, but lose the message? Mr. Destiny thinks you did his evil bidding, the crew members don't connect the firing to the union, and everyone's happy."

"Except the person who got fired."

"True. But I'm sure I'll recover quickly," said Thomas.

"You'll recover—you're volunteering to get fired?"

"It's the only way."

"You can't do this," she said.

"Vanessa, we're so close. Help me. Help me do this, please."

Vanessa's lips pressed together and a wrinkle appeared on her forehead. "How could it look like you were being fired for something else?"

Thomas thought fast. "All we need is a rumor. If one of the crew sees me do something that's grounds for instant termination, they'll spread the story to the rest of the crew. They'll think I got fired for that, not for organizing."

"Won't Mr. Destiny hear about it?" said Vanessa.

"Not likely. He pays as much attention to crew members as that horse does." Thomas pointed to the horse head.

Vanessa laughed in spite of herself. "All right. Let's say I take you up on this crazy plan. What can I fire you for?"

"Safety. If I do something unsafe, I have to be fired."

"So you have to do something unsafe, in front of me, where other crew members can witness it?" said Vanessa.

"Then they spread the story of why I got fired, yes," said Thomas. "But Mr. Destiny will think it's because he told you to fire someone."

"This is insane," said Vanessa.

"I'm open to other options," said Thomas.

Vanessa threw her hands up in the air. "You know as well as I do there aren't any. What will happen after? Will you appeal to get your job back?"

"Of course. And if that doesn't pan out—well, I'll find something. After all, we toasted to new beginnings, didn't we?" He poured all his charm into a teasing smile.

"You—" she started. "You're insufferable."

"But you like me anyway," said Thomas.

## CHAPTER 19

*Vanessa*

The crisp, clear fall sky would have been a joy to behold, if the election deadline weren't bearing down like a hurricane.

A hurricane would have suited Vanessa's mood better.

She went over the plan in her mind, one more time, but could find no fault.

The opening move: to get Dirk out of the way.

She tracked him down in the underground break room.

He sat at one of the wobbly tables with a pile of papers and a pen—which was strange, because there were perfectly good desks in the Legacy office.

She approached the table. "Dirk."

He scrabbled the papers together and rested his arms on top.

Vanessa caught a glimpse of blank and completed fields on the top paper. "I need you to cover the parade today."

"Sure, sure," said Dirk.

She could tell he was eager to acquiesce and get rid of her. *Fair enough. It's mutual.*

With Dirk taken care of, she removed her nametag and ran upstairs to the Coffee Garden. Two Vietnamese iced coffees in hand, she retreated to the Legacy office.

"I got us some coffee," she said to Charlotte in a sing-song tone. Vanessa held out one of the iced coffees and wiggled it from side to side as if it were dancing in midair.

"You know what I like," said Charlotte. She reached for the coffee.

Vanessa pulled it back slightly. "Come in my office."

"What are you on about?" Charlotte looked at Vanessa with amused suspicion.

Vanessa said nothing, but brandished the coffee one more time, with a slight smile.

"Fine," said Charlotte. "Be mysterious." She stood up and followed Vanessa into her office.

Vanessa closed the door and handed Charlotte a coffee. "Things are about to—how shall I put this?—hit the fan. I can't explain exactly what's happening, but I need you to just roll with whatever happens. It may get weird before it's all over."

"You're asking me to trust you and roll with it without knowing what's going on?"

"Yup," said Vanessa.

Charlotte stirred her coffee. "And you're compensating me for this with an iced coffee?"

"No, the iced coffee is because I need someone to share my bad habits."

Charlotte laughed. "All right. I'm in. Promise me something, though."

"Anything," said Vanessa.

"Someday, you have to tell me the whole story," said Charlotte.

"Charlotte, if I make it through this in one piece, I'll spare you no detail."

"You promise?" said Charlotte.

"Cross my heart," said Vanessa. She checked the time. "And now I must go. I need to walk through the attractions."

"Have fun out there," said Charlotte. "Try not to get fired! I'd miss you. And the free coffees."

Vanessa went to Ghost Factory first. She made a show of inspecting each station, from the front entrance to the unloading area, before moving on to American Dream. At American Dream, she confirmed that Dirk was in place for the parade while performing a walkthrough of the entrance, the lobby, the theater, and the break room.

Her hands felt cold and her heart skipped the occasional beat as she departed American Dream for Gold Rush.

She walked to the overlook.

The mine trains dove and swerved just as they always had.

Vanessa remembered her training day with Thomas and smiled to herself. *Once more unto the breach.*

There was no turning back now.

She forced herself to walk at a normal pace down to the attraction entrance, where she made small talk with the crew member stationed there before following the inner hallway to the break room, and then, at last, to the loading area.

Thomas stood at the controls, his Gold Rush hat rakishly tilted as usual.

She gave the control tower a cursory inspection, carefully avoiding eye contact with Thomas.

A train filled with visitors returned to the station with a roar. One crew member triggered the mechanism to open the gates to allow the visitors to exit the train. Another crew member directed visitors to the exit. A third crew member began filling the empty train with visitors.

*Three witnesses. Here we go.*

She approached the train with a fist aloft, the signal to "hold" the train. The gates swung closed in front of her. She leaned slightly over the gate as if to check a safety bar and let her fist drop slightly.

The train launched.

Vanessa whirled around. "Why did you send that train?" she shouted at Thomas. "I was signaling to hold!"

The crew members stared.

Thomas, eyes wide, stuttered his response. "I thought you dropped the hold signal."

"I most certainly did not. You could have killed someone," she said.

The next train came in, but none of the crew members moved—they were too busy watching the show.

Vanessa looked around, as if realizing for the first time that their exchange took place in full view. "Wait for your station replacement, then come to my office immediately," she said, then stormed out.

Alone in the stairwell leading underground, she leaned against the wall and felt tremors ripple up her stomach. Her knees shook involuntarily. The brief but intense scene had sent adrenaline coursing through her.

*At least it's over.*

Thomas would report to her office, she would alert Mr. Destiny, and it would be done. She took a deep breath and resumed her walk downstairs.

## Thomas

The Voice of Destiny floated through the underground halls as Thomas walked up the corridor to the Legacy office.

*Goodbye, Voice of Destiny. You only said what you were told to say.*

He ran his hand along the wall.

*Goodbye, strange underground maze.*

He shifted his gaze ahead.

*Goodbye... Dirk?*

Thomas and Dirk traveled a collision course, both en route to the Legacy office. They arrived at the office door at the same time.

"Dirk," said Thomas.

"Thomas," said Dirk.

They both reached for the door handle.

Dirk flinched back.

Thomas pulled open the door and allowed Dirk to precede him into the office. Charlotte seemed to be making a valiant attempt to look studious, refusing to look up when Thomas and Dirk entered.

Thomas knocked on Vanessa's door.

"Come in," she called.

He shut the door behind him. "Dirk is right outside," he whispered.

She came around the desk to stand face to face with him. "We need to sell this," she whispered. "In case he talks to Mr. Destiny."

Thomas raised his voice. "What do you mean, you're letting me go?"

Vanessa nodded. "That's it," she whispered.

"I'm going to miss having a manager like you," he whispered.

"I'm going to miss having an employee like you," she said quietly.

He gazed into her eyes. They stood so close to one another that he could feel the warmth radiate from her. He leaned down. "Can I ask you something?"

She nodded.

"If—hypothetically speaking, of course—we were no longer in a manager-employee relationship, would it be out of line to request the pleasure of your company on a date?"

Her smile bloomed. "Hypothetically speaking, I think it would not be out of line," she whispered. Her fingertips brushed against his.

Thomas laced his fingers through hers. "Then fire me," he murmured.

Vanessa raised her voice for Dirk's benefit. "I'm sorry, Thomas. There's nothing I can do."

Thomas lifted his free hand and slowly brought it to Vanessa's face, brushing her cheek as softly as if it were a delicate rose. "You are amazing," he whispered.

His next sentence was loud enough to be heard outside Vanessa's office. "This is totally unfair!"

Vanessa echoed his movement and placed her hand along his jawline, drawing him forward.

Her lips touched his cheek with the softest kiss.

"Until we meet again," she whispered.

# CHAPTER 20

## Vanessa

The day of the union election dawned with a flurry of activity. Representatives from the union set up a voting station underground, watched by observers from the Destiny Park management team.

The relentless Voice of Destiny ceased broadcasting music, and instead chirped a looping monologue to encourage crew members to "Vote no!"

Upon arriving in her office, Vanessa found a note left on her desk, marked "To Vanessa from Dirk."

*Meet me this morning at the Comet Lounge.*

She refolded the missive and tossed it on her desk.

Why would Dirk want to meet in a lounge in Galaxy?

Vanessa examined the note one more time before carrying it to Charlotte. "Any idea why Dirk would send this?" asked Vanessa.

Charlotte took the note and read it. "He's running off to Galaxy on election day?" she said. She handed the note back to Vanessa. "That doesn't seem like Dirk."

"It doesn't make a lot of sense," said Vanessa. She tossed the note in the trash.

"By the way," said Charlotte, lowering her voice before continuing, "Thomas told me what happened."

"Did he?" Vanessa smiled softly as she drifted into a recollection of the touch of his hand.

Charlotte eyed her. "Judging from the look on your face, maybe he didn't tell me *everything* that happened."

Vanessa cleared her throat, then patted her hair as if it had gone out of place, which it hadn't. "Well. I should—I should get back to work." She turned to go back to her office.

"If you can concentrate," muttered Charlotte.

"I heard that," Vanessa said.

Back in her office, Vanessa tried to concentrate.

Charlotte was right.

She couldn't.

"I'm going to see what Dirk is up to," she said to Charlotte.

Charlotte snickered. "I knew you couldn't concentrate," she said.

"Judge not, lest ye be judged," said Vanessa, clipping her radio on.

"Wouldn't dream of it. I hope I find somebody who has that kind of effect on me," said Charlotte, fanning herself.

Vanessa laughed. "I'll keep an eye out." She exited the office and went upstairs, crossing through Discovery on her way to Galaxy.

She passed the solar system Ferris wheel before encountering The Black Hole restaurant and realizing she'd overshot her destination.

The entrance to the Comet Lounge hid in a corner behind a group of shrubs trimmed in abstract geometrical shapes.

Vanessa skirted the planter and entered a revolving door. On the other side, the revolving door opened to a lounge with dark red carpet. The polished black bar against the far wall contained rows of bottles and glasses laid out in sparkling order.

A black grand piano dominated the center of the lounge.

Vanessa looked around for Dirk, finding only a bartender and a man dressed in formalwear leaning against the bar, facing away from the door.

She approached the bar and slid onto a stool.

"Can I get a virgin Bloody Mary, please?" she asked the bartender, then glanced down the row to the gentleman in formal clothing.

It was Dirk.

"Hello, Vanessa," he said, rising from his seat and moving to one next to her. "One for me, too," he said to the bartender.

"Dirk?" She stared at his outfit.

"I have some news," he said.

The bartender slid their drinks across the bar.

"I'll say," said Vanessa. She lifted her drink and sipped from its salted rim.

"I am officially transferring," said Dirk.

"Transferring? But you just got here," said Vanessa. "You're not going back to Fantasy?"

Dirk shook his head. "Not that kind of transfer. I'm changing roles." He drummed his fingers along the edge of the bar in a rhythmic pattern.

"You're drumming your fingers"—she looked from Dirk to the grand piano in the center of the room and back again—"you're playing the piano?"

"Welcome to my office," he said.

"No kidding?" Vanessa's eyes widened. "Congratulations," she said, and meant it.

"You'll have to come by for a show sometime," he said. "Bring friends. Or a date."

Their gazes met.

He smirked and raised one eyebrow.

"I'll do that," she said, wondering what he knew.

He held his glass aloft. "To new beginnings," he said.

Vanessa clinked her glass with his, sealing their détente.

---

At the end of the day, Vanessa pulled her union-free binders off the shelf and left for the Mirror Castle.

She passed the voting station outside the underground break room, where observers from both sides counted and recounted the ballots.

Crew members on break gathered around to watch.

The Voice of Destiny droned on above it all.

At the Mirror Castle, she shifted the binders into one arm to allow her to push the elevator buttons with her free hand.

She approached the desk of Mr. Destiny's secretary.

"I need to return these," she said.

Voices echoed from Mr. Destiny's office.

"I paid you all this money and we still didn't win!" said Mr. Destiny.

Vanessa heard the sound, but not the content, of the consultant's response.

Mr. Destiny spat a final "Get out!"

The door opened and Amy strode through, head held high.

"I can see he's busy," said Vanessa as she handed the binders over to the secretary. "I'll just leave these with you."

Vanessa hurried back to the elevator, where she and the consultant waited for the elevator in silence.

They stepped inside.

"So … the crew members got their union?" asked Vanessa.

"You win some, you lose some," said Amy with a shrug. "I get paid either way."

The elevator dinged and the doors opened. Vanessa allowed Amy to precede her, then stepped into the sunshine beneath the Mirror Castle.

Though it was time to go home, Vanessa didn't want to leave.

She scanned the crowd, an automatic habit for a theme park manager, noting the crowd size and movement, picking out the positions of the crew members in the streets, absorbing the energy and reading it like tea leaves.

Something in the air set her path for the manager parking lot, where she retrieved a spare set of street clothes.

She changed in the locker room and emerged in the Fantasy bazaar, inconspicuously attired, with no name tag to be seen.

The scent of caramel corn led her to the stand where she purchased a bag for herself. She continued down the row until she reached the outdoor stage.

Vanessa slid onto a bench and fished around in the bag for

the choicest-looking pieces of caramel corn while waiting for the show to begin.

She had just popped too many into her mouth when she heard a familiar voice above her.

"Is this seat taken?"

Thomas stood before her. She shaded her eyes to look up at him. He wore fitted jeans topped with a black turtleneck sweater, sunglasses, and a fedora. On anyone else, it might have looked absurd.

On him, it was charming.

She swallowed hastily. "Have a seat," she said. "How did you get in here?"

He sat down next to her. "I bought a ticket like everyone else," he said. "No way I was going to miss my weekly show."

"We probably shouldn't be seen together," she said. She offered him caramel corn.

"Probably not," he agreed, reaching into the bag.

"I heard you won the election," she said.

He threw his head back and laughed. "Poor Mr. Destiny," he said.

"Poor, poor Mr. Destiny," said Vanessa.

They grinned at each other.

"Wait—you've got something—right there," said Thomas, staring at Vanessa's face.

Vanessa colored. "What? Where?"

"A little caramel. Right there. Let me—" He leaned forward and kissed her on the lips. "It's gone now," he said.

She leaned back and cast an appraising gaze at him. "Smooth," she concluded.

"Oh, you have no idea," he said, his eyes twinkling.

"Maybe not," said Vanessa. "But I'd like to find out."

## Pomegranate Champagne

Toast someone you love with this ruby-colored sparkler!

### Ingredients:
Champagne
Pomegranate juice
Pomegranate arils

All ingredients should be completely chilled.

### Instructions:
1. Pour champagne into a flute, leaving space at the top to add a shot of pomegranate juice.
2. Pour a shot of pomegranate juice into the flute.
3. Garnish with a teaspoon of pomegranate arils and serve immediately.

## Author's Note

One of the most enjoyable parts of writing fiction is making up wildly improbable scenarios, like a manager falling in love with a union-organizing employee and secretly taking his side against her boss. Although this story is entirely a work of fiction, many of the union-busting tactics described in Roller Coaster Romance are based on reality. Union-busting tactics are not an artifact of the past; they affect workers around the world to this day.

If you'd like to learn more about the history and methods of union-busting, I recommend reading *Confessions of a Union Buster* by Martin Jay Levitt with Terry Conrow. It's currently out of print, but used copies are easily found online.

Pick up *"They're Bankrupting Us!": And 20 Other Myths About Unions* for a highly readable introduction to what unions do, and the origins of common misperceptions about unions.

To learn about workers' rights and organizing strategies, I suggest reading *Labor Law for the Rank & Filer* by Staughton Lynd and Daniel Gross, and *Win More Union Organizing Drives* by Jason Mann.

For a fascinating true story of undercover union organizing, check out *Playing Against the House* by James D. Walsh.

–K.M.

## About the Author

Kate Moseman is a writer, photographer, and recipe developer who lives in Florida with her family.

Did you love Roller Coaster Romance?
Leave a review on Amazon!

Made in the USA
Middletown, DE
06 July 2024